THE KILLING OF EMILIANO SALA

The Inside Story of a Tragic Transfer

By Harry Harris

EMPIRE
PUBLICATIONS

First published in 2020

EMPIRE PUBLICATIONS
1 Newton Street, Manchester M1 1HW
© Harry Harris 2020

ISBN: 978-1-909360-72-3

To the pursuit of the truth

CONTENTS

ACKNOWLEDGMENTS

IN UNRAVELLING the complexities of the death of Emiliano Sala I would like to thank Mercury PR's George Tucker, journalist Ben Rumsby, who brought me on board to the *Telegraph*'s Investigative team as a consultant, and his 'team-mate' Tom Morgan.

Thanks also to Ash and John at Empire Publications.

ABOUT THE AUTHOR

HARRY HARRIS is a double winner of the British Sports Journalist of the Year award, who has successfully investigated football corruption, including producing dossiers on two former England managers.

Harry was presented with the British Variety Club of Great Britain Silver Heart for "Contribution to Sports Journalism", is a double winner of the Sports Story of the Year award, the only journalist to win the Sports Story of the year accolade twice. He has a total of 24 industry awards, a number related to his investigations into the murkier side of the Beautiful Game.

A regular football analyst on TV news and sports programmes; he has appeared on programmes as diverse as Richard & Judy and Newsnight. A regular on BBC News, ITV News, Sky, Setanta. Radio 5 Live, Radio 4, and TalkSport, Harry has been interviewed on Football Focus and was part of the original Hold The Back Page and Jimmy Hill Sunday Supplement shows on Sky.

He is arguably the most prolific writer of best-selling football books of his generation. Among 85 books are the highly acclaimed best seller in the UK and the States "Pele - His Life and Times" . Other books include: "Gullit: The Chelsea Diary", "All The Way Jose", Chelsea Century, Chelski, ˜Wayne Rooney - The Story of Football's WonderKid" and his most recent book: "Liverpool: Diary of the Season." He has ghost-written autobiographies of Ruud Gullit, Paul Merson, Glenn Hoddle, Gary Mabbutt, Steve McMahon, Terry Neill, Bill Nicholson and George Best's last book, "Hard Tackles and Dirty Baths". Biography subjects include Roman Abramovich, Jurgen Klinsmann, Sir Alex Ferguson, Jose Mourino, Terry Venables, Franco Zola and Luca Vialli.

One of the most influential football columnists for three decades, Harry remains one of the best investigative journalists and news gatherers of his generation having worked for the *Daily Mail*, *Daily Mirror, Daily Express, Daily Star, Sunday Express*, *Star on Sunday,* ESPNsoccernet and BT Sport.

Harry has also directed four documentaries on Ossie Ardiles, Kenny Sansom, Kerry Dixon and Ron "Chopper" Harris.

INTRODUCTION

O N JANUARY 21ST 2019, EMILIANO SALA WAS killed when the light aircraft he was returning to Cardiff in crashed into the English Channel. I use the word 'killed' advisedly because such has been the intrigue surrounding his death that there is more than a suspicion of foul play. In fact the subsequent police investigation into criminality has so far arrested just one man, later released without charge.

The fall-out has been unprecedented in English and French football. Besides police enquires into manslaughter, an allegation of murder and death threats investigated by the South Wales and Metropolitan forces, there have been allegations of fraud, a FIFA hearing and an appeal to the Court of Arbitration for Sport (CAS) as Cardiff City refuse to pay Nantes the agreed £15m transfer fee pending legal action for alleged negligence by the owners of the plane as well as ongoing aviation and criminal investigations. Two people are also serving custodial sentences for posting images of the footballer's dead body online.

The key figures in this tragedy were brought together by the usual driving force in most football transfers these days: money.

EMILIANO SALA was a 28 year-old Argentinian striker who had played for eight clubs during a peripatetic career. He dreamed of a career in one of the big leagues in Europe when he arrived in France to play for Bordeaux as a 20 year-old before being loaned out to several lower league French clubs and signing for Nantes for £1m in 2015. There Sala's career stalled once more, registering 12 goals in successive seasons before a change of manager saw him hit a hot-streak during which he scored a dozen goals in as many games. By the start of December 2018 he was joint top scorer in Ligue 1 alongside French wonderkid Kylian Mbappé and was firmly on the radar of clubs desperate to sign a striker in the all-important January transfer window.

WILLIE McKAY is a football agent who made his fortune acting as a go-between for English clubs wishing to sign French-based players. As we shall see, McKay had no desire to 'babysit' Sala, he merely wanted to get him a big money move to Premier League strugglers Cardiff City. McKay and Cardiff boss NEIL WARNOCK had a good working relationship and as far as the Scot was concerned the deal suited all parties: Nantes would get an inflated fee for a striker they bought for just £1m a few seasons earlier,Cardiff would get the striker they desperately needed in their bid to stay in the richest league in the world and Sala would get a huge increase in wages and the fame and glory of potentially saving the Welsh club from dropping into the Championship and Mr McKay would earn himself an easy ten percent...

The go-to pilot for Willie McKay was DAVID HENDERSON, who has since been arrested and is under investigation for manslaughter. For that fateful flight he passed the assignment on to DAVID IBBOTSON, who remains missing presumed dead. Ibbotson was colour blind so shouldn't have flown at night and he himself admitted he was 'rusty' with the plane's landing controls. Ibbotson was in fact a part-time gas fitter and DJ who was flying illegally for the agent who booked the flight – Willie McKay. McKay later confessed that he covered the costs of the flight yet the pilot did not possess a commercial licence. Ibbotson had several County Court judgements against him, the last coming only a couple of weeks before he accepted the offer to take Sala to France and back in a 35 year old single-engined Piper Malibu plane.

The death of Emiliano Sala is one of the most bizarre and tragic events to have blighted the world's favourite sport. This book addresses some of the key questions: what really occurred on that fateful day? What role did McKay, Henderson, Warnock and the executives of the two clubs play that led to the crash? What does this transfer say about the manner in which clubs conduct their transfer business?

The contents of this book may change your perception of the murky world of football and the sinister forces behind the scenes culpable for the player's death. It was certainly chilling when a toxicology report pronounced that both pilot and passenger would have been exposed to dangerous levels of carbon monoxide and had possibly been dead before the plane hit the English Channel. This led into an investigation into the ownership and upkeep of the plane which again shed light on the murky business of passenger ferrying on small, privately owned planes. It is a huge grey area affecting fast-moving sports such as horse racing and football, particularly during the bi-annual transfer window as the deadline nears.

A year on, the Sala family are no closer to discovering the truth, having hired one of the UK's most dogged QCs to represent them in forthcoming High Court legal battles. However suspicion and rumour run wild with Sala's cousin Martin Gatti one of many who sensed foul play from the outset, "They can't say a plane just crashed and they both died and that's it! I have seen many irregularities from the beginning."

Reading like a paperback crime thriller, the inside track on the death of the Bluebirds Legend who never got to play for his new club is one of the most intriguing football stories of all-time. The Sala story is told in full here with unrivalled access to the facts through sources close to the figures at the centre of one of the most astonishing events in football. If this plot had been submitted as a work of fiction it would have been thrown out as being far-fetched!

I was involved in the *Daily/Sunday Telegraph* Investigative team that broke the story that a negligence case was being considered with potential litigation against Nantes and Cardiff's subsequent refusal to pay any of the £20m in fees and agents commissions. It is Cardiff's contention that when Sala stepped on that plane to return to Wales he wasn't legally a Cardiff player.

This is a forensic examination of all the facts to probe exactly why Sala's former girlfriend believed that a 'football mafia' was at work and why she wasn't so far from the truth… It is a story that unfolded in South Wales, Western France, Argentina and Zurich and will almost certainly end up in the High Court in London.

The book shines a light into the murky corners of football and shows how deals are done, corners are cut and men make their money. The methods used by the clubs and agents in this book are similar in a lot of transfer deals, the only difference here is that a tragedy has allowed the world to see how certain parties operate.

One source close to the investigations asked me: "Is this a manslaughter case or was it murder?" Perhaps the wreckage of the plane should have been salvaged so we could have learned more about how carbon monoxide leaked into the cockpit yet the Air Accidents Investigation Bureau (AAIB) opted against this and an inquest in November 2019 was told that the wreckage at the crash site had now been 'washed away' following a scan of the area, so perhaps we'll never know the truth.

I have been a football journalist for many years, I have investigated many issues and you sense when there is something important to investigate. That's how I felt from day one following my initial contact with an agent and his stinging response; it was clear that this story was worth looking into. I had already worked with Ben Rumsby on another case and it was quickly decided that this was something we should look into further and the results were alarming. What you read here are the established facts that we could put into the public domain. There was much more we couldn't print for legal reasons. Some facts were hard to check and cross check; there is a lot more that will emerge in this case.

The *Telegraph* broke the story of the alleged death threats against four of the Cardiff City hierarchy by the football agent, Willie McKay, who was deeply involved in brokering the transfer and facilitated the fatal flight. The South Wales Police handed a file to the Metropolitan Police who investigated the allegation of death threats made in the capital and issued a warning to the agent to desist. In the case that occurred in London, McKay personally confronted one of his victims. Having established where he lived the Glaswegian former bookmaker stalked him and accosted him outside a café near his home before delivering his gangster threat. Willie McKay denies he has been sent a restraining letter by the Met. However, there are allegations McKay ignored police directives in subsequent tirades. Remarkable details of the threats were published by the *Daily & Sunday Telegraph* as part of its series of blockbuster exclusives, which form some of the detail within this book in which McKay claimed that Cardiff City had a vendetta against him and were 'throwing him under a bus'.

This book puts the events of Sala's death into context as they unfolded. In addition, I have obtained hitherto unseen documentary evidence which adds further insight into the events of the abortive club record £15million transfer.

This is by far the most chilling and explosive book I have written on football. For me it is the most intriguing of all the 80 plus books on football I have written in 40 years as a journalist. Little wonder there has been interest in turning this book into a documentary film.

Harry Harris

CONTRAT D'AGENT SPORTIF

Entre les soussignés

La SASP FC NANTES au capital de 500 000 euros, immatriculée au RCS de Nantes sous le n° 388 113 276, dont le siège social est situé Centre Sportif La Jonelière 44240 La Chapelle sur Erdre, représentée par Monsieur Franck KITA, dûment habilité, en qualité de Directeur Général, ci-après dénommée le « Club »,

Et

Monsieur **Mark MCKAY**, gérant de la société MERCATO SPORTS LTD, immatriculée sous le n°10683175 dont le siège social est situé Martin Grange Lodge, Martin Common, Doncaster, DN10 6DD, mandataire sportif autorisé par la FFF à exercer sur le territoire Français, ci-après dénommée l'« Agent »,

Ci-après dénommées conjointement les « Parties »

PREAMBULE

Le présent contrat est conclu conformément et dans le respect des articles L222-5 à L222-22 et R222-1 à R222-42 du code du sport.

Monsieur Emiliano SALA, né le 31/10/1900, de nationalités italienne et argentine (ci-après le « Joueur ») est lié par un contrat à durée déterminée avec le Club jusqu'au 30 juin 2022.

Plusieurs clubs anglais du championnat de football de Premier League on fait part de leur souhait d'obtenir la mutation définitive du Joueur pour la saison 2018/2019

L'Agent a développé une connaissance, une expertise et un savoir-faire dans la mission de négociation de contrat de mutation de joueur de football.

L'Agent se voit ainsi confier, la mission de négociation de la mutation définitive du Joueur dans un club de football duc championnat de football de Premier League.

IL A ETE CONVENU CE QUI SUIT

ARTICLE 1 : OBJET

The contract between
Mark McKay and Nantes

1: THE PLAYER

EMILIANO SALA IDOLISED ONE OF ARGENTINA'S greatest goalscoring centre-forwards, Gabriel Batistuta, so when he was told he could get his break in the Premier League and fulfil his dream to be like his hero and join a club in one of the big European leagues, he jumped at the chance. Unfortunately, like most aspects of this sad story, things weren't quite as they seemed. Indeed, nothing that occurred subsequent to receiving that initial letter of intent to take him to the glory trail of money, prestige and glory in the Premier League, turned out to be what it seemed. For this is a tale of modern football and its tawdry and underhand ways – as they saying goes, all that glitters is not gold…

Born on 31 October 1990 in the small rural community of Cululu in the Santa Fe province of Argentina, about 340 miles north-west of Buenos Aires, Emiliano Sala Taffarel grew up watching Batistuta's heroics. Batigol's World Cup performances and his finesse in front of goal for Fiorentina led Emiliano to dream of wearing the same number 9 shirt for his country in which his hero had scored an incredible 56 goals in just 78 appearances. Sala wanted to become a prolific goalscorer at the highest level and to that end he left home in Argentina at just 15 to pursue his dream.

Sala had played for his local club, San Martín de Progreso, from the age of 5, graduating through the youth ranks until he was selected to join a football school called Proyecto Crecer some 90 miles away in San Francisco, Córdoba which was directly affiliated with Spanish club RCD Mallorca and French side FC Girondins de Bordeaux. It proved a tough task to gain recognition in his homeland, at a time when there was a profusion of outstanding Argentine goalscoring talent, so Sala took the giant step and moved to Europe in a bid to make take the next step up the football ladder but having failed to force his way into the Bordeaux first team he was loaned out to other French clubs.

However if Sala was short of superstar ability everyone who met him had nothing but good words to say about the amiable Argentine. Felipe Saad, who played with Sala at one of the clubs he was loaned out to Caen, told *L'Equipe* after his death, "He was a lovable, generous fellow. He always believed that football was a team sport. I am so shaken. His move to Cardiff was going to bring him the recognition he deserved, albeit belatedly. He so deserved his talent to be recognised". Sala was loaned out to three different French clubs - US Orleans, Niort and Caen, scoring a total of 42 goals in 87 games. At Niort, in Ligue 2, his then-coach Pascal Gastieu said of him, "I considered his technique to only be adequate, though everything else was there but he was a generous guy and when he was on the field he never gave up. He knew he had room for improvement, especially on a technical level. He'll reach full maturity later than the average player, you'll see." The player agreed with this assessment, commenting, "My headers aren't good enough, even though I'm tall. It's something I'll have to work on."

From time to time his agent offered the striker to a number of Italian teams (Sala had an Italian passport) but they all rejected him. At the age of 23 he was still referred to as a budding talent; two years after moving to Europe he was given a run in the Bordeaux first team but scored just once in 12 games and was loaned out to Caen for the rest of the season where he scored five times in 13 games to help keep the Normandy team in Ligue 1. That summer Sala got his big break, a £1 million, five-year deal that took him to Nantes. The 6 foot 3 inch centre-forward was a name that hardly registered in English football; his progress was slow, but he was making an impact at last, at least in France.

In January 2016, after just a handful of appearances and a few goals, Wolverhampton Wanderers, then in the Championship, made an approach for Sala. Nantes President Waldemar Kita, who had signed the Argentinian, rejected the 4 million Euro offer which would have quadrupled his original 1 million euro investment. Clearly Nantes believed in the player and Sala admitted he was tempted by the Molineux club even though they were in the second tier of English football. Yet the Argentinian knew that, even at 26, he wasn't yet mature enough to go up against the defences he would face in English Championship football. "I haven't left my mark on Nantes yet" Sala commented at the time, "if I was to leave, I would want it to be after I've made it, and I'd want to leave a good memory."

Sala scored a dozen goals in each of the next two seasons before suddenly and totally unexpectedly hitting a hot streak for Nantes. In the summer of 2018 there had been a deadline day approach from Turkish giants Galatasaray. He was out of favour with then manager Miguel Cardoso, who wanted a more technical brand of football but the Portuguese coach was forced to reassess as Sala suddenly improved in front of goal. Between July and September, during the Cardoso era at Nantes, Sala scored four times. Cardoso was sacked in October and under new boss Vahid Halilhodžic he scored eight times up until he left the club in January 2019. This included a hat-trick in the new boss's first game.

After such a stop-start career, it was little wonder that Sala was tempted when the opportunity arose to move to the Premier League on the back of this rich vein of goalscoring form, for he had very fortunately hit his straps at just the right time and came to the attention of a number of clubs battling relegation in the richest league in the world. Sala was flying as the year ended. He stood third in the Ligue 1 scoring charts with 12 goals ahead of esteemed company such as Paris Saint-Germain duo Edinson Cavani and Neymar! The only names in front of him were French wonderkid Kylian Mbappé and Nicolas Pepe, who eventually signed for Arsenal for £72m in the summer of 2019.

Unlike those around him in the top scorers list, Sala wasn't easy on the eye; gangly and awkward looking, he was not particularly technically gifted, but he had other strengths. He was strong in the air, he was a penalty box poacher and had a tremendous spirit and determination. He knew how some looked down on these qualities. Replying to his critics Sala told reporters, "I'm someone who's really honest, and it doesn't bother me at all. I've got my style, it's my nature, I'm not going to change, I'm Argentine! Being on the field, giving everything for myself and maybe scoring a goal, and seeing a friend or a member of my family happy in the stands, that's what makes me happy"

As 2018 ended and the January transfer window opened, Sala's stats were impressive enough to interest a few managers in the Premier League, especially one desperate for a quick-fix goalscorer amid a relegation battle. According to Opta, Sala had scored eight goals from 12 big chances. His conversion percentage stood at 66.67%, which was sixth in Ligue 1 in terms of players with at least five goals; higher at that time than big names such as Lionel Messi (64.29%), Harry Kane (52.94%), Cristiano Ronaldo (50%) and Mbappé (50%).

In total he had scored 42 goals for the Breton club, and as his profile began to grow in France he came to the attention of Willie McKay who knew that his old friend Neil Warnock, manager of Cardiff City, was on the look out for a striker and in urgent need of some goal power if his team had any hope of surviving in the Premier League in their first season after guiding them to promotion.

"Emiliano, My name is Willie McKay …
We are not interested in looking after your personal interests."

The intervention of Willie McKay was about to change Sala's life. The ubiquitous Scot had plied his trade as a successful wheeler-dealer, ducker and diver in the football economy for many years. He'd had notable successes and no few controversies, including being banned as a football agent in France but not to worry, his son Mark would take the reins for this deal, Willie was just acting in an 'advisory capacity'.

McKay senior had became accepted within English football as the go-to agent for relatively little known players in France, and he operated from the off-shore tax haven of Monaco. Willie could play the game; he promised Sala that clubs of the stature of Everton, West Ham and Fulham were interested in him and pointed to stories to that effect in the English press. In the end it turned out that the only deal that ever got remotely serious was with Cardiff City and his old mate Neil Warnock.

McKay sent Sala a personal letter, as he was intent on helping his son Mark pull off a deal for Sala as he found his feet as a football agent. The Scot needed to tie Nantes to a contract, and knowing they were strapped for cash, he persuaded them that he could pull off a good deal. The Scot had contacted his old pal Neil Warnock and offered to take the Cardiff boss and his assistant on a scouting mission to watch Sala in Nantes.

The ball was rolling…

Those who knew Emiliano Sala described him as a warm, sensitive fellow who lived a quiet life off the pitch. French football writer Erik Bielderman wrote the following profile of him on the BBC website after his death.

"The transfer marked belated recognition for a player who might have been imperfect technically but who was physical, courageous and endearing. On the pitch he was confrontational; off it he led a quiet life. He loved detective novels and would never go to an away game without taking a book. He played the guitar too but took that up quite late, and usually preferred to leave it at home. A common morning sight in Nantes was Sala, seated at a table outside a café with his Labrador Naja curled up at his feet.

"There was no doubt his technique still lacked something, but the Premier League looked like his turf to conquer. He was initially unsure about joining a club struggling in their own league, but Kita, the president of Nantes, didn't want to miss out on the 17m euros transfer fee.

"Rumour had it that Sala didn't really want to leave for Cardiff. His coach, Vahid Halilhodžic, had rekindled his career last

October following a long period of struggle under former manager Miguel Cardoso and refused to discuss the possibility of his striker leaving. Halilhodžic - himself a former centre-forward at Nantes - had decided his mission was to re-launch the Argentine player, whose role model since childhood had been the legendary striker Gabriel Batistuta.

"'He's a sensitive young man; he needs to feel confident, so the priority was to help him believe in himself. Only after that could we talk, striker-to-striker,' said Halilhodžic.

"Sala confirmed: 'The club was ready to sell me to Galatasaray, but I held on tight. I have no regrets, because Vahid and I talk a lot, and I'm steadily improving.'"

Bielderman continued, "Sala was first and foremost an instinctive striker. If he were an English player, he would have been Jamie Vardy: a player who liked wide spaces and being part of a team with a strong counter-attacking style; a lively, light player but one who was also resilient and reliable - a real South American warrior. During his time with French club Niort he was often referred to as 'the local Carlos Tevez'. Sala was also a skilled 'fox in the box', thanks particularly to his exceptional finishing ability with his head. He had perfect timing, and he was clinical on set-pieces with his great headers. The player Cardiff wanted was the Sala that Halilhodžic had so successfully polished and relaunched."

At the time of his ascent into the upper echelons of the Ligue 1 scoring charts, Nantes president Waldemar Kita said of Sala, "He's a polite, nice, adorable boy, adored by everyone" but at the age of 28 he was pretty long in the tooth, particularly for the big Premier League clubs. Back in the heyday of agents like Willie McKay, a 28-year-old striker who had hit a hot streak in France would have been much more valuable. There would have been more bidders from under pressure managers near the Premier League drop zone wanting a short term quick fix. However a recent trend had seen elite clubs pay ever-larger fees for young players who would they could grow into their long term team building strategy. These targets are typically selected by Directors of Football with an eye on the long term rather than managers trying to save their skins with a quick fix.

As it was, McKay went straight to Sala to gain the player's agreement to sell him, informing him that he had a mandate from his club Nantes. The email is reproduced here in full:

Emiliano,

My name is Willie McKay. First of all, I tried to reach [your agent] Meïssa [N'Diaye] by call and SMS in the last few days without success. We are not interested in looking after your personal interests; finance, holidays. Baby-sitting is not our market. We do transfers - to this date, over 600 from Didier Drogba and Anelka to Payet, Seri, Anguissa. A lot. Let us tell you how we operate and how the Cardiff City situation came around because you must be wondering. We will explain. We work for clubs in France including PSG, Marseille, Lyon, Nice, Lille, Toulouse, Le Havre, Nantes and others, for players to be transferred to England. In your case we have spoken to every club, including Manchester, Chelsea, Liverpool. We think eventually you could play in these clubs.

We approached Nantes, as we do for many players at other clubs, to get the authority to sell. We don't try and cross the player's agent. Some are very happy to work with us. Some get very jealous and protective. With all the shit they say - like 'he is like a brother to me' and 'he is like my son'. In reality, if you were not a footballer these people don't care about you. They only care about money. That is the truth because that's all we care about. That's why we like to work for clubs - no emotion, simple business. That's it!

In your case, we begged Nantes for the mandate. I think they were curious of what your value was because you scored last year and this year without any offers for you. Because you are a very good player and we only target very good players. But as you said in one of your interviews some clubs like you and others don't.

We have had West Ham, Everton, Leicester, Burnley, Fulham and Cardiff watching you at Nantes and away matches. We take our plane get clubs in it - people who can decide, not the local scouts. For different reasons; age, style of play, playing in League 2 and other issues, we only have an offer from Cardiff City, newly-promoted with a manager who fell in love with you first of all from your footage online. Then he has watched you twice: once in Rennes and against Marseille in Nantes with his assistants, nearly five weeks ago. Neil Warnock will have all his players with one objective: get the ball to you.

He sees you as a typical English centre forward, like Drogba, Alan Shearer. He told me you will score easier in his team than in Nantes, because all your teammates in Cardiff will play to your strengths. He would like to meet you. Either they will fly you over in their jet to look around or they will come to meet you in Nantes. You can bring whoever you want, just to give you an idea. They will pay you around £50,000 per week gross plus bonuses on a 4-5 year contract and whoever you bring with you, be it Meïssa (who has done nothing) or your mother, who can also represent you by law in England. She could receive around £1 million in sterling for herself.

Here is a club who really wants you and believe in you as we do and if a big club comes in for you while in Cardiff they will not stand in your way. Cardiff is a great place to live. My sons live there. The support are very loud. They never stop singing. In my experience, I think if you don't try the Premier league in England where the game suits you, you will regret it. Cardiff have been told you don't want to go there. That's probably our fault. It was us who put in the media about other clubs wanting you - West Ham, Everton etc, to create an interest in you. That's what we do. It can be misleading for the player himself, but unless we do this most people would not know you because nobody follows the French League.

I hope this explains everything to you. If you need any other help or questions you want to ask please do. Cardiff can have a jet for you tonight or tomorrow to pick you and any other people you want to bring with you. You don't need to sign but at least hear what they have to say.

The Player

Regards, Willie McKay

This email sheds light on how agents such as McKay ply their trade. By tipping off close associates in the media about interest in a player they inflate a player's value in the transfer market. There are plenty of columns to fill and gossip of this nature during the transfer window, especially in January when the elite clubs tend not to be as active. It is food and drink to some reporters who are eager for an easy story: a tip-off from the likes of McKay can make life much easier for a reporter with column inches to fill and a deadline to meet and if the transfer doesn't come off, no one seems to mind too much as it is deemed ˜gossip'.

In the case of Sala, the facts tell a very different story to the fake news peddled by McKay. No one was that interested in the player aside from Cardiff City but the column inches generated suggesting that a handful of clubs were willing to negotiate whetted the appetite of Cardiff City. Instead of being a player no one wanted, Sala looked like he had several suitors which of course forced the transfer fee up and with it McKay's fee.

Four months later conclusive evidence emerged to support the theory that Sala did not want to join Cardiff City, and was being forced out of Nantes. The French club were desperate for cash and Cardiff were the only possible destination but Sala asked his agent to find him "somewhere better".

A WhatsApp message to a friend on January 6 indicated that he was not keen on the move. The message was revealed on a L'Equipe Enquete documentary on French television.

> *"Last night, I sent a message to Meïssa [N'diaye, Sala's agent], he called me a few hours later. So we had discussions and he told me the last night Franck Kita [son of Nantes owner Waldemar] sent him a message to talk, so he called him. They spoke. And, they want to sell me. So, there is the offer from Cardiff today. On their side, they have negotiated to get a lot of money. So they absolutely want me to go there.*
>
> *"It is true that it is a good contract but from a football*

perspective it is not interesting for me. So there you go, they are trying in every way to get me to go there. Me I am not scared to go there, because I have battled throughout my career, so to go there and fight, that does not make me scared.

"On the contrary. But also, I say to myself that Meïssa must find me something better between now and the end of the window. Meïssa has said no to Cardiff because he does not want me to go there. He thinks that in terms of football, in terms of where we are today, we are in a position of strength in every which way, in terms of on the pitch, the contract, all of that.

"But I don't care about that and I do not want that. I don't give a f*** about being in a position of strength. It is true that I would like to find something interesting in terms of contractually and also from a football perspective, but sometimes you can't have both. On the other hand, I do not want to speak with Kita, because I do not want to get angry. He is someone who disgusts me when I am face to face with him.

"Him today, he wants to sell me to Cardiff because he has done a super negotiation, he will get the money he wants, eh? He, he wants me to go there, he hasn't even asked what I want! All he cares about is money. So, today, we are like that. A complete mess. So there you go! I don't know.

"I don't know what to do because as I said to you it is I who has to get up every day and see the face of this person. But nobody is looking at me! Myself? Me internally, what I am having to go through. So, it is very hard, it is very hard, because I feel like there are not many people who would put themselves in my place."

When his signing was announced, Sala made all the right noises as you would expect. He was hardly going to sign for the club then denounce a move he didn't actually want! Players are traditionally gushing about their new clubs when comments from them and their club are posted on the official social media site. At the time Sala said he was relishing the opportunity to prove himself in the Premier League and was set to make his debut against Arsenal. "I'm very happy to be here," he told Cardiff's official website, "it gives me great pleasure and I can't wait to start training, meet my new team-mates and get down to work." In a later tweet, he wrote: "I know the challenge is big, but together we will make it." No doubt that was perfectly true, but it hid a multitude of doubts that have since come to light.

Sala had a positive attitude and he wanted to make his mark in English football, and maybe, as McKay had told him, he would catch the eye of one of the league's elite clubs. Reacting at the time his father Horacio, a truck driver back home in Argentina, said "you know what it is to play in the Premier League. He never thought he'd reach that level. It's crazy!"

However the player was hiding the truth that he had been forced out of Nantes and forced to join a club he didn't want to play for. So when it later emerged that there had been a hitch in the contract he signed, and the reality was that he wasn't actually a Cardiff player when he stepped inside that plane on January 21 as negotiations were still on-going, there were clearly a lot of people connected to that big money transfer who had a lot to lose if the deal fell through...

2: THE MANAGER AND THE AGENT

NEIL WARNOCK IS A WILY OLD FOX. HE'S BEEN in the game for so long there isn't a trick in the book he doesn't know about football management. As for the intricacies of the transfer market, he is one of the old school hands-on managers; he knows what he wants in terms of a player and what he can do for his team, and he knows how to go about getting him.

Warnock is a veteran of some of the trickier aspects of the managerial game, he's seen it all before. He possesses an uncanny knack in getting his teams promoted to the Premier League and in all he has guided 8 teams to promotion, a British record. He has been hugely successful and sought after for that particular trick of his trade. When Birmingham City scored a third goal against Fulham on the final day of the season 2017-18, as Cardiff were seeing out a dull goalless draw with Reading, it all but confirmed Cardiff's promotion to the Premier League.

As that news filtered through it sparked the expected celebrations, with hundreds of supporters pouring on to the pitch before the final whistle. "The Blues are going up" was the chant from the Cardiff fans who made up the vast majority of an exuberant 32,478 crowd, a record for the Cardiff City Stadium. In the directors' box, owner Vincent Tan couldn't have been more delighted, as the Premier League was the holy grail of financial reward and represented a chance for his players and fans to rub shoulders with the game's elite.

Warnock's eighth promotion surpassed the records of Dave Bassett, Jim Smith and Graham Taylor. The Yorkshireman had started his managerial career by taking non-league Scarborough into the Football League back in 1987. He said of the record "It's my greatest achievement getting this group of lads promoted. The best one by a mile. If you knew what I've had to do off the field as well as on the field, you'd understand."

From relegation to the Championship in 2014, he had led Cardiff back into the big time after just 18 months in charge. "The fantastic thing is the fans are proud of being a Bluebird again, everybody wants to come and support the club, I know we're not easy on the eye, but I'm really proud of building a team capable of ruffling a few feathers."

Promotion was one thing, staying in the Premier League would be another matter entirely. "Yeah it's going to be hard. We'll be odds-on to go down! Hey ho. Why worry, we've got there. You're going to enjoy it. I'm looking forward to it. And if it goes pear-shaped I'll just leave."

Having banked a very handsome bonus for gaining promotion, one of football's longest-serving bosses knew that the activity in the summer transfer window wasn't sufficient to keep Cardiff City afloat in the games loftier heights among the likes of the Manchester clubs, Liverpool, Spurs, Arsenal and Chelsea.

Yet the first few months of the new Premier League season told Warnock that his best chance of survival depended on whether he could buy an out-and-out goalscorer, the Bluebirds having scored just 19 goals in 20 Premier League games by the end of 2018. As early as November Warnock was already deep into research on his targets during the January transfer window to avoid a repeat of his summer frustration when he missed out on Chelsea's Tammy Abraham in August when a late bid failed and the England forward joined Aston Villa on loan for the season. While a striker was top of Warnock's January wish-list he was also targeting a full-back and a central midfielder.

By then his old pal Willie McKay had recommended Sala and organised two flights to ensure that the Cardiff manager watched the striker personally. Oddly, though, McKay introduced Warnock to the Nantes president. Often managers like to watch prospective targets unannounced rather than tip off the selling club that they're interested.

Warnock was familiar with McKay's modus operandi, they had

worked together on several deals in the past. The Scot always tried to make life as easy as possible for his clients by sorting out private flights. Often McKay would brag, "I'll fly you out in *my* plane" but it turned out to be more bravado than reality and McKay was hiring the planes and paying the pilots, no doubt without paying much attention to whether the pilots were registered adequately for commercial flights as his normal pilot Dave Henderson was licensed so it was not an issue.

Warnock crossed the Channel twice on McKay chartered flights to watch Sala and in hindsight it was quite a harrowing experience for the Cardiff boss to think back on how the Scot had organised his travel to Nantes in a private plane, just as the agent did for Sala's fateful flight. "I'd been on a couple of planes like that," Warnock later confessed, responding to a question about whether he had flown on the single-engine Piper PA-46 Malibu aircraft, "I think the ones I'd been on might have had two engines, but I'd been over to Nantes a couple of times and I think I had that pilot, who I thought was a fabulous pilot. So I just can't comprehend it."

Willie McKay was clearly hands-on, although the mandate to sell was actually contractually with the company in the name of his son Mark, as McKay senior was banned from transfer business in France and would have been barred from acting in this way under the terms of his bankruptcy agreement. Willie would later describe his motives for direct involvement as 'nepotism' as he tried to aid his son Mark in gaining a foothold in the world of football agents. Both Mark and Willie worked for Excelfoot, a Glasgow-based agency which went into liquidation into 2017. Mark was now listed by Companies House as a director for two real estate businesses: Bawtry Sports Village Ltd and Bawtry Leisure Park Ltd, along with his girlfriend Rachel Morse, with whom he was regularly seen in pictures shared on the pair's social media pages.

The McKay family had worked with Cardiff and Warnock in the past. Indeed at one time two of Willie's sons were at Cardiff and one of them remained there throughout the Sala scandal. Twin sons Jack and Paul McKay came through the youth ranks at Doncaster where the family had moved having been based in Monaco for years. Both were now 22 and moved to Leeds United before a January 2018 switch to Cardiff. Paul is a centre-back who moved on loan to Morecambe until the end of the 2018-19 season. Jack, a striker, was still in the Bluebirds' Under-23 side.

Following trips to watch Sala in action and watching several hours worth of footage of him, Warnock had made his mind up to sign the Argentinian but he still had to gain authorisation from the club's four-man transfer committee. The committee met at a variety venues, depending on the members' availability. Sometimes in London, where chairman Mehmet Dalman had his offices, at the club itself or via conference calls. Made up of chairman Dalman, CEO Ken Choo, senior director Steven Borley and manager Warnock, they would decide on whether to go for Sala.

Mehmet Dalman has a long standing football background. Cardiff City's urbane chairman is an investment banker specialising in finance and the mining industry but professional football has been in his life since he had trials for Crystal Palace when he was 18 and he was involved in the Glazer takeover of Manchester United. The Turkish-Cypriot financier has many footballing anecdotes, arguably the best is how he flew to Libya by private jet to discuss a deal to buy-out John Magnier and JP McManus's 29.9% shareholding in United with Colonel Gadaffi's key advisors in 2004 after the Irish tycoons fell out with manager Sir Alex Ferguson over ownership of the racehorse Rock of Gibraltar and asked Dalman to dispose of their shares. Gadaffi, who died in 2011 during a revolutionary coup, bought Italian club Perugia instead after the parties failed to agree on a price for the controlling stake in the Old Trafford club. Dalman was also an adviser to the Glazer family, now owners of United, who at that time had a 20% stake in the club which was under Dalman's control, in addition to the 2.5% stake he held.

The Cardiff chairman has also been banker to former owner of the *Express*, Richard Desmond and was the first non-German to sit on the board of Commerzbank before bowing out as Head of Investment Banking after seven years to set up his own asset management firm.

Football was his first love and he is a season ticket holder at Old Trafford, the club he has supported since he was a boy living in Cyprus. Dalman joined the Cardiff board in January 2012, initially taking the role of chairman in July 2013 with the intention of dedicating a couple of days a month to the position, but it proved to be hugely more time consuming. Dalman confirmed Cardiff were aiming to bring in "three or four" new signings during the January transfer window on the day Warnock's team were thumped 5-1 by Manchester United in Ole Gunnar Solskjaer's first game in charge. The Norwegian had been Cardiff boss the last time the Bluebirds had been relegated from the top flight four years earlier.

"We are focused on what we need to do," Dalman said at the time, "we would like to bring in three or four players, although our search for a striker is not so far going as well as we would like. Neil Warnock is the best manager we have had during my time at Cardiff City and we work closely together. Look at our team, we are not that far away. Yes, a little bit more quality is needed but we can bring that in during January."

Yet behind the scenes the Cardiff City chairman was concerned about the proposed Sala deal. Having seen deals come and go he had an intimate knowledge of the murky world of agents and wasn't convinced the price was right for a player aged 28 who had not been on any English club's radar as far as he knew, while there had been scant coverage of Sala in the English press until very recently. Dalman was too long in the tooth to be fooled by a few recent newspaper snippets linking Sala to a series of clubs, whereas only a few months before no one appeared to be interested. Not only that but the Argentinian had one year left on his contract after that season and Nantes were yet to offer him a new deal which was a give away that either the player didn't want to stay at the club or the club were trying to offload him. Above all, nothing suggested that Sala was in a hurry to leave Nantes.

Then there were the profusion of agents. Mark McKay, his father Willie, the player's French agent Meïssa N'Diaye, who also represented Benjamin Mendy, Michy Batshuayi, and Cardiff's Sol Bamba, and the suspicion in all of these cross board transfers that other agents had a piece of the player. Then there were the usual concerns whenever Premier League clubs tried to sign players from South America that there might be lingering third-party ownership problems. Third-party ownership is illegal in the Premier League and that tends to lead to extra expense and possible litigation. The deal didn't sit well with Dalman.

The committee had considered as many as 100 players over a period of months. These were whittled down to around 25 as the club knew it had to act in the January window and it was now or never to make a big decision on how to invest their limited resources with three players high on the agenda and a striker the main priority.

Clearly Warnock was sold on Sala and he made a powerful case to the board that a goalscorer of his type would be effective in the Premier League, and how his goals might be enough to keep Cardiff in the Premier League. Dalman and the committee watched a video of some clips and his goals, and yes he seemed to be in goalscoring form, but he also looked "clumsy", according to Dalman. He didn't look like a £20 million striker to him.

They also looked at two English strikers as alternatives. They had been quoted a price of £10m for Watford's Troy Deeney in the previous window but quibbled at his £100,000-a-week wage demands yet the package for him was cheaper than the total package for Sala and here was a player proven in the Premier League. It was a comparison that was brought up in discussions.

Despite all these misgivings, Warnock made it clear that Sala was the one that he wanted and it was almost accepted that the manager had the casting vote should any doubts be expressed. Still Dalman felt so strongly that he made his opposition firmly known in correspondence inside the club in internal emails.

Above all, the price being quoted for Sala didn't make sense to Dalman. He felt it was far too high for all the reasons he had given. Frankly, he smelled a rat! His suspicions were confirmed about Nantes being strapped for cash and anxious to sell as Mark McKay had confided as much to Ken Choo because, as the agents were stressing, part of any agreement was to stack the payments top heavy from the start, while Cardiff were sticking to scheduled payments of equal proportions spread over three years. From what everyone knew about Nantes president Waldemar Kita there was good reason to tread carefully.

In fact Dalman's misgivings become more agitated in a number of internal emails, gaining in strength and conviction each time he hit the send button. His message was clear; he did not think it was worth "breaking the bank" to get Sala and that other targets, some cheaper, some more expense, should be given greater consideration.

When it came to the four-man committee casting their vote to give the go-ahead it was usually done by a majority vote, the outcome was 3-1 in favour of signing Sala. Dalman voted against. This was the first and only time he had voted against signing a player at the Transfer Committee. The chairman valued the player at between 10 and 12 million euros, and his advice was to walk away from the deal unless Nantes came to a far more reasonable valuation. Dalman could sense that Nantes were desperate for the money, and were anxious to cash in on Sala, especially now they had found a Premier League club willing to buy. To that end, Dalman negotiated the price down quite considerably as Nantes were in fact asking for 18 million euros plus a 6 million bonus should Cardiff remain in the Premier League. He got it down to 17m and 3m, the bonus for survival spread out over three years.

As it transpired, Dalman had good cause to have concerns about the financial issues. Cardiff were enraged that Willie McKay had tried to push up the player's price by planting stories in the press. As has been established, McKay's email to Sala listed several prominent Premier League clubs, while Wolves were also reported to be keen. However the Scot was dismissive of Cardiff's suggestions that he inflated Sala's price through media stories, which he insisted had always been part and parcel of the transfer business, and therefore an accepted custom which those in the industry would be well aware; sending a message to a club to alert them that a player might be available is not the same as that club showing an interest or chasing the player, let alone being prepared to make an offer. It is all smoke and mirrors.

In the aftermath of the crash and with the role of McKay coming under greater scrutiny and Nantes already instructing their lawyers to pursue payment of the first instalment of the transfer fee, Cardiff's lawyers contacted the clubs mentioned in the planted stories to establish whether they ever had a genuine interest in the player. I contacted some of the clubs and their responses shed some light on how McKay manipulated the market. On my request for the strength of the club's interest in Sala, West Ham co-owner David Sullivan emailed back, "We were interested, but thought the price was high for a guy who'd only done it for one season. Sometimes strikers are one season wonders. I then asked the co-chairman who is hands on with the Hammers transfer business whether he would have agreed with the valuation, and what price would he have valued Sala at. The answer was £8m due to high risk, but how do you value any player?"

Burnley's Technical Director emailed back "There was no interest. Just another player put forward by the agent like 2,000 others. Nothing of note." While a high level source at Fulham texted back "I have checked for you and am told - and asked to pass onto you - that it was a total invention by agents. FFC had already purchased Mitro (Aleksandar Mitrovic)."

Yet, in the contract between Nantes and Mark McKay's company Mercato Sports Ltd., that confirmed the Scot's right to sell the player, it states "Several English clubs in the Premier League football championship have expressed their desire to obtain the player's definitive transfer for the 2018/2019 season".

SPORTS AGENT AGREEMENT

Between the undersigned:

FC NANTES SASP [professional sports limited company] with share capital of €500,000, registered in the Nantes Trade and Companies Register under no. 388 113 276, registered office Centre Sportif La Jonelière, 44240 La Chapelle sur Erdre, represented by Mr Franck KITA, duly authorised, in his capacity as Managing irector, hereinafter referred to as the "Club",

And:

Mr **Mark MCKAY,** managing director of MERCATO SPORTS LTD, registered under no. 10683175, registered office Martin Grange Lodge, Martin Common, Doncaster, DN10 6DD, sports agent authorised by the FFF to operate in French territory, hereinafter referred to as the "Agent",

Hereinafter jointly referred to as the "Parties"

WHEREAS

This contract is concluded in accordance and in compliance with Articles L222-5 to L222-22 and R222-1 to R222-42 of the French Code of Sport [*Code du sport*].

Mr Emiliano Sala, born 31/10/1900, of Italian and Argentine nationality (the "Player"), is bound by a fixed-term contract with the Club until 30 June 2022.

Several English clubs in the Premier League football championship have expressed their desire to obtain the Player's definitive transfer for the 2018/2019 season.

ie Agent has developed knowledge, expertise and know-how in negotiating football player transfer agreements.

The Agent is therefore engaged to negotiate the final transfer of the Player to a football club in the Premier League football championship.

THE FOLLOWING HAS BEEN AGREED

CLAUSE 1: PURPOSE

The purpose of this agreement is to lay down the terms and conditions under which the Agent shall perform a negotiation and assistance engagement on behalf of the Club under the terms and conditions set out below.

FC NANTES

☆ ☆ ☆ ☆ ☆ ☆ ☆

Registered office: Centre Sportif LA JONELIÈRE - 44 240 LA CHAPELLE SUR ERDRE • **Postal address:** BP 31124 44 311 NANTES CEDEX 3
Tel: 02 40 37 29 00 - Fax: +33 (0)2 40 37 29 21 - E-mail: contact@fcnantes.com
SAS [simplified limited company by shares] with share capital of €500,000 - 388 113 276 NANTES TRADE & COMPANIES REGISTER - VAT FR 49 388 1 13 276

The agreement between Nantes and Mark McKay for the sale of Sala to "the English Premier League championship" following interest from "several English clubs".

Emiliano Sala

@EmilianoSala1

There is a new Sala in town
@premierleague

Very happy to sign here
@cardiffcityfc
!! I know the challenge is big but together
we will make it

Impatient to discover the league & the team
#BlueBirds

*Emiliano Sala poses with the Cardiff shirt on the day he
signed for the Welsh club, 19th January 2019, smashing the
club record transfer fee in the process.*

3: THE TRANSFER

AFTER DAYS OF SPECULATION, EMILIANO SALA 'signed' with Cardiff City on Saturday January 19. The usual photo shoot took place with the player paraded with a Cardiff shirt smiling alongside CEO Ken Choo. The local press were happy to peddle the line that Neil Warnock had beaten off a number of clubs in signing a striker who had scored 12 goals in 19 Ligue 1 games in 2018/19. The manager did little to dispel the theory and supporters were left with the impression that the Bluebirds had pulled off a coup. One thing was certain, Warnock had desperately wanted the player and he had got his man, and he was about to milk the moment for all it was worth.

It was only later, when Willie McKay's role in the transfer and Warnock's acquiescence in how the Scot used the media was revealed, that the truth emerged. For now it seemed a pretty routine transfer acquisition and a big step up for a club like Cardiff City who broke their transfer record in the process.

Sala was pictured arriving at the Cardiff City Stadium in the Welsh capital before heading back to France. The player posted a picture on his Instagram account with his former Nantes teammates as he said goodbye to his ex-colleagues at their training ground. "La ultima ciao," were the words he added to his Instagram post before boarding that fateful flight. "The final goodbye."

Remarkably, despite Sala tweeting a picture of himself with his team-mates back in the dressing room to say his goodbyes, which was re-tweeted by Nantes themselves, the French club later claimed that they knew nothing of his return to their club to be pictured with his team-mates! Nantes' argument was that they had no idea when the picture on social media had actually been taken.

Sala had signed a four-and-a-half year contract worth £50,000-a-week to mark his late arrival into the big time with a Premier League club. Nevertheless the player was determined to

make a go of it and if he maintained his French goalscoring form he might attract the attention of the top clubs. He met some of his new Cardiff team-mates and spoke again with manager Neil Warnock at the training ground. He was scheduled to take his first training session on the Tuesday but 'Emi', turned down his new manager's offer to join the squad for their game in Newcastle because he wanted to dash back to put his adored Labrador in kennels and say his final farewells to his Nantes team-mates with whom he had formed such a close bond. Warnock did not object to this request, it is something that haunts him to this day.

That evening Sala sat in his Cardiff hotel room alone waiting for confirmation from the club of scheduled BA flights. Cardiff had offered a range of options, including taking a train from Cardiff to Heathrow for a flight to Paris Charles de Gaulle and an onward train to Nantes, or flights via Amsterdam. However, on the morning Sala 'signed', Cardiff club secretary Michelle MacDonald asked

Willie McKay if airport-to-club transport had been organised, and McKay was later keen to prove that conversation took place by producing his mobile phone records. When it became too hot for McKay after the tragedy unfolded, he was at pains to illustrate that the club were aware that an option was for the agent to sort out the transport as Sala was struggling with the timetabling of scheduled flights.

McKay later argued that he paid for six flights to help Cardiff City and released the details of these to underline his point. He twice paid for manager Neil Warnock's flights to Nantes to see the player, once with assistant manager Kevin Blackwell. He twice paid to fly Sala and his agent Meïssa N'Diaye on return flights to Cardiff, once to view the club and once to 'sign'. McKay, rather than Cardiff, arranged transport from airport to club on those two visits. McKay was keen to show that it wasn't unusual for him to arrange and pay for private flights, and produced a dossier of information which he pushed out to the media.

5 December 2018
The first flight – Stapleford to Nantes

A day after Cardiff City lost 3-1 to West Ham at the London Stadium, Neil Warnock, Kevin Blackwell, Mark McKay and Willie McKay boarded a flight organised and paid for by Mark to Nantes. On arrival they met Marseille's director of football Andoni Zubizarreta at the French team's hotel in Nantes to discuss two Marseille players who could be available in the January transfer window. After this meeting they went to the Nantes match early to meet the club's president. Nantes won 3-2 with Sala scoring one and setting up another. Afterwards they all returned to the UK. Warnock and Blackwell disembarked at Cardiff before the plane continued to Stapleford in Essex to drop off the McKays.

6 January 2019
McKay arranges for Warnock to meet Sala

Willie McKay sent an email to Emiliano Sala. The player's French agent, Meïssa N'Diaye, called Willie and agreed for Sala to meet Warnock after Nantes played Montpellier on 8 January. The McKays arranged a flight with Warnock, Mark McKay, Willie McKay and Cardiff's player liaison officer Callum Davies on board. They all went to the match where Sala was said to have played "really well" and "better than he had in the Marseille match". Sala and a friend met Warnock at a hotel in Nantes. Warnock invited both N'Diaye and Sala over on the following Monday to see Cardiff's stadium and meet the club's chief executive Ken Choo to discuss terms. They all flew back to Cardiff on the morning of 9 Jan 2019, with the flight paid for by Mark McKay.

14 January 2019
Sala flies to Cardiff

A plane picked up N'Diaye in Paris, then took him to Nantes to pick up Sala and continue to Cardiff. N'Diaye went to the stadium to look around and talk about a contract. The same day they returned to Paris via Nantes; Sala left the plane in Nantes, while N'Diaye carried on to Paris. The plane returned to Guernsey where it is based. All paid for by Mark McKay.

18 January 2019
Sala transfer agreed

Mark McKay liaised with Cardiff's club secretary Michelle MacDonald, on the instruction of club CEO Ken Choo, to gain confirmation that the transfer fee has been agreed. He informed Ms MacDonald that Sala would be arriving at 9.10am by plane to Cardiff for his medical, to be registered in time for the Newcastle match. Ms MacDonald asked him whether arrangements were made for Sala to be picked up at the airport. He told her he had planned to pick up Sala himself. Sala arrived at Cardiff Airport around 9.30am and the pair headed to Cardiff City's stadium where they arrived at around 9.50am. They were greeted at the stadium by Davies and joined there by N'Diaye half an hour later, following his arrival in the UK on a scheduled flight from Paris. The McKays organised a plane for N'Diaye for around 3.30pm so he could get back to Paris for important meetings. Cardiff City booked a hotel and Sala went there in the early evening after passing his medical and signing the remaining paperwork. The McKays were staying in the same hotel and, having been joined by Jack McKay following training earlier in the day, they all returned to the hotel accompanied by Davies. Messages were then exchanged between Sala, Jack McKay and Willie McKay. The McKays arranged a flight, of which Davies was aware, on the Friday night to depart on Saturday morning. The flight left at 11.30am on 19 January and Sala returned to Nantes. The pilot, David Ibbotson, waited two days for Sala to finalise his business in Nantes before departing Nantes for Cardiff on Monday evening so the footballer would be back for training on Tuesday morning.

21 January 2019
The day of the crash

Sala was due to be met by Davies, who was waiting for him to arrive at the Signature Flight Support building at Cardiff Airport on Monday evening. Willie McKay later claimed Cardiff City knew about the flight and who organised it. McKay's stance is that Cardiff had a logistical dependency on him down to their inexperience in signing a big-money overseas player. He argues that the first flight to Nantes for Warnock – from Stapleford airfield in Essex after the away match at West Ham on December 5 – included an initial meeting with Marseilles' director of football Andoni Zubizarreta. This was to discuss two of his club's players, before talks with Nantes' president Waldemar Kita about Sala. The

French clubs then played each other with Warnock and Blackwell looking on. McKay wanted to demonstrate that Cardiff were so pleased to have him working for them in the transfer window that he did groundwork on two other possible deals for Warnock, who was said to be interested in midfielder Bouna Sarr and striker Konstantinos Mitroglou, both at Marseille.

However Cardiff argue that Mark and Willie McKay were working for Nantes; they had a mandate from the French club and were to be paid a 10 per cent cut of the fees received by Nantes. The contract specified it was incumbent on Mark McKay to ensure the transfer fees were paid. Therefore in the furore that followed the crash, Cardiff viewed the McKays as agents of Nantes, the club who had mandated him to find a buyer for Sala, and particularly cited French law which would make an employee liable, even the activities of its consultants. Therefore the allegation that McKay was representing Nantes in booking the fateful flight and that the French club were therefore responsible for it formed one of the core aspects of Cardiff City's legal case handled by the club's lawyer Chris Nott at Capital Law.

Back on that fateful Friday night, Sala's tricky travel logistics were resolved when he received a text from one of his new team-mates, albeit a reserve, the son of Mr Fix-It himself. Jack McKay jovially suggested that his dad would sort it all out with a private flight, and that if he helped Jack to score for Cardiff City, then everything would be free of charge!

The messages between Jack McKay and Emiliano Sala

Friday, 18 January

7:43pm - Jack McKay: 'My dad has told me that you are going home tomorrow. He could organise a plane to take you direct to Nantes and to come back on Monday, at a time that suits you, so you can get to training on Tuesday.'

7:51pm-Emiliano Sala: 'Ah that is great. I was just in the middle of checking if there are some flights to get to Nantes tomorrow.'

7:56pm–McKay: 'He said he could organise a plane that would go direct to Nantes.'

7:56pm– Sala: 'How much will it cost?'

7:56pm–McKay: 'Nothing. He said if you help me to score goals it's nothing.'

7:59pm–Sala: 'Hahaha with pleasure.'

8:00pm– Sala: 'We are going to score lots of goals.'

8:01pm – Sala: 'I want to leave tomorrow for Nantes at around 11am and come back on Monday night around 9pm to Cardiff if that is possible.'

8:05pm –McKay:'Good. I'll send a message when that's sorted.'

Sunday, 20 January

5:00pm – McKay: 'Hi there is it possible you could come back at seven in the evening on Monday night? Just because the pilot has to get home in the north after he gets to Cardiff.'

5:01pm – Sala: 'Hi, half past seven would be possible.'

5:03pm – McKay:'Yes that's good.'

5:05pm –Sala: '[PICTURE OF LUGGAGE] Can you ask if I can bring this on the plane?'

5:06pm –McKay: 'Good yeah.'

5:07pm – Sala: 'But is that going to be OK for the plane?'

McKay: 'Yes there is space on the plane for your luggage.'

5:12pm – Sala: 'OK.'

Monday, 21 January

4:16pm – McKay: 'I'm going to call in a moment.'

4.23pm –McKay: 'He said that it is the same company.'

4.27pm – Sala:'OK thanks.'

Jack McKay's decision to release the text messages to the BBC, who were organising an exclusive interview with Willie McKay at the time when the going was getting tough for the Scot, was done so without the club's permission, and that did not go down well at all with the Cardiff hierarchy. The fact that Jack was later loaned out to a club nearer his dad's home back in Doncaster when the dust settled probably tells its own story! Jack completed a loan move to Chesterfield "looking to be closer to his family". The 22-year-old never made an appearance for Cardiff's first team. Paul McKay had already joined Morecambe on loan on 4 January 2019.

Willie's footballing twins, Jack and Paul McKay, both 22, had been on the books of Doncaster Rovers and Leeds United having started their football education in France and had offers to go to other academies but settled at their hometown club when they were 16. Jack is a striker who spent time out on loan with a Scottish League One outfit Airdrieonians, while Paul plays at centre-back. In 2016 Leeds United signed the twins, then aged 19, for undisclosed fees on two-and-a-half-year deals from Doncaster Rovers. In mid-January they joined Cardiff City after a short trial with the Bluebirds' Under-23s.

Willie's other son, Mark, was following in his dad's footstep as an agent and became the 'official' agent acting for Nantes in the sale of Sala but that mandate expired on February 2, so he had precious little time to make sure Sala was sold in the January transfer window. Mark is credited as helping West Ham sign Dimitri Payet from Marseille in a £10.7m move in 2015 and he is also credited with representing former Everton midfielder Idrissa Gana Gueye but it was clear that Willie was the man with the contacts to ensure the deal would go smoothly.

Willie McKay is one of the best known agents. He has pulled the strings behind numerous transfers, bragging he has been involved in as many as 485 deals ranging from Ronaldinho's move from Paris Saint-Germain to Barcelona to acting for Queens Park Rangers during negotiations to sign Joey Barton on a free transfer. He has represented Barton, Charles N'Zogbia, Ross McCormack, Pascal Chimbonda and Amdy Faye but his career has

Cardiff City's Player Liaison Officer, Callum Davies

not been without moments of controversy. McKay was one of five men arrested on suspicion of conspiracy to defraud and false accounting in November 2007 as part of the City of London Police football corruption probe. He was cleared of any wrongdoing 18 months later. In December 2008, he was given a suspended ban by the FA for breaching regulations by acting for two different clubs in two consecutive transfers of Portsmouth and Manchester City striker Benjani. Mark McKay also followed in his father's footstep of having his ups and down in the agency business. He was the director of the Glasgow-based company Excelfoot Ltd., which went into liquidation in 2017

Senior club officials at Cardiff claim that they only became aware a private flight had been arranged after they were alerted by the club's Player Liaison Officer Callum Davies that Sala had failed to arrive at Cardiff airport as planned on Monday evening, emphasising that they had not known of the details of Sala's travel arrangements.

WhatsApp messages show how Cardiff did offer a commercial flight. Screenshots of messages between Sala and club Player Liaison Officer Callum Davies later appeared in French media outlet *Ouest-France*. They showed Davies offering Sala a commercial £82 Flybe flight from Cardiff Airport to Paris Charles de Gaulle as part of the proposed journey to France and back. According to the messages - written in French and Spanish - the Argentinian player informed him that Willie McKay had contacted him and he no longer needed help. Davies, who attended the player's funeral

Sala tells Cardiff City's player liaison officer
that Willie McKay had been in touch.

in Argentina, was the man who raised the alarm when the plane failed to arrive at Cardiff Airport, where he was due to meet him.

A WhatsApp message shows Cardiff City offer Emiliano Sala a commercial flight

Callum Davies, Player Liaison Officer: [thumbs up emoji]

Emiliano Sala: Thank you very much

PLO: It's nothing friend. I write Spanish better than I speak it

ES: Ha ha very good

PLO: My girlfriend speaks Spanish. She is a teacher [shares commercial flight details]

PLO: It is an option perhaps. Cardiff-Paris. But it's early.

ES: Friend. It's good. I have a flight going tomorrow to Nantes and

Willie McKay (second left) and son Jack (left) pose for a picture with Mark (third in) and Paul McKay (right)

return Monday night to Cardiff. Willie McKay called me.

PLO: Ok mate. Have you agreed a price with him?

ES: Yes it's good. We will speak tomorrow before leaving for Nantes.

PLO: Ok that works. What time do you fly?

4: THE FATAL FLIGHT

"I'm here on a plane that looks like it's about to fall apart"

EMILIANO SALA WAS HAPPY, RELAXED AND animated during the Sunday lunch thrown in his honour with his Nantes team-mates on the day before he would board that fatal flight back to Wales. For days, ever since he knew he was going to be a Bluebird, he was constantly in touch with former Manchester United full back Fabio Da Silva who also had a spell with Cardiff City but had joined Nantes in July 2018. Emi was hungry for information about his new club and life in the Welsh capital. Fabio told Sala he had loved life in Wales and that he too would also love the city, the people, the football and life in the Premier League.

However Sala told Nicolas Pallois, the team-mate who drove him to the airport for his flight back to Cardiff, that the trip to Nantes from Cardiff "had been bumpy and he feared his safety for the journey back". Pallois asked him to text him when he arrived. Sala had flown on a number of occasions courtesy of Willie McKay without mishap and they had been very comfortable journeys, so he would have no reason to feel nervous when he boarded the flight from Cardiff to Nantes. However for that flight he found himself in a different plane with a different pilot and got a nasty shock of a very bumpy landing, with a pilot who later admitted to a friend on Facebook, "Was not too bad when I got there, but I'm a bit rusty with the ILS (instrument landing system)."

Yet Sala looked happy enough in the hours before take off; posting pictures with his former teammates on social media. On one he poignantly wrote "the last goodbye!"

Sala, though, had a secret he dare not share with anyone; his lavish new £50,000-a-week contract was invalid. The paperwork had been returned by the Premier League. The manner in which the signing on fee payments were scheduled were declared to be a breach of Premier League regulations, as it later emerged that Nantes had insisted on clauses that resulted in the Premier League returning the documents and informing Cardiff they had to be redefined, maybe even renegotiated, so they refused to register him, and he would be unable to play in his debut scheduled for the Arsenal game. Technically at this point Sala could have signed for another club, he could have changed his mind and returned to Nantes. All things were possible. He could, of course, have accepted new terms and conditions suited to the Premier League rules. However it is Cardiff's contention that at this point Sala was not their player.

These issues were surely on Emiliano Sala's mind as he strapped himself into his seat aboard the Piper PA-46 Malibu, a 35 year-old single turbine engine aircraft, piloted by part-time DJ and gas fitter David Ibbotson. He was flying into the unknown on all fronts – a strange plane in which he'd had a 'bumpy' ride on the way over to France and towards a club where he was not yet officially a player. They were soon flying at an altitude of 5,000ft.

Shortly after take-off at approximately 7.30 pm, Sala sent a WhatsApp voice note message to some of his family and friends:

"Hello, little brothers, how are you crazy people?

"Brother, I'm dead, I was here in Nantes doing things, things, things, things and things, and it never stops, it never stops, it never stops.

"I'm here on a plane that looks like it's about to fall apart, and I'm going to Cardiff, crazy, tomorrow we already start, and in the afternoon we start training, boys, in my new team."

"Let's see what happens, so, how are you brothers and sisters, alright?"

"If in an hour and a half you have no news from me, I don't know if they are going to send someone to look for me because they cannot find me, but you know… Dad, how scared am I!"

At 8.15pm, as the plane passed Guernsey, the pilot "requested descent", but Jersey air traffic control (ATC) lost contact with the plane while it was flying at 2,300ft.

At 8.23pm the plane vanished. The Guernsey Coastguard received an alert from Jersey ATC that a light aircraft had gone off their radar approximately 15 miles north of Guernsey, sparking a huge rescue operation.

Back at Cardiff airport Callum Davies, the club's Player Liaison Officer, was waiting for Sala. When the plane hadn't arrived at the appointed time he contacted the authorities. Davies had liaised with the player for several weeks before the Argentinian striker boarded the private flight organised by agent McKay. He was the Cardiff City member of staff who formed the closest relationship with Sala and was one of just three Cardiff employees who attended his funeral in Argentina. Manager Neil Warnock and chief executive Ken Choo were the others.

Davies left the club on September 5, 2019 citing family reasons, after six years working at a club he had joined immediately after graduating from university. Fluent in French and a Spanish speaker, Davies was a popular member of staff at Cardiff, where his departure came as a surprise. The players were told that he had chosen to leave as his wife had been offered a job in Dubai, where he was now looking for work.

On Tuesday, January 22, at 2am, the search was called off "due to strengthening winds, worsening sea conditions and reducing visibility".

At 8am, the search resumed by which time French aviation authorities named Sala as one of those on board the plane. The French civil aviation authority also confirmed the pilot of the plane was David Ibbotson, from Crowle, near Scunthorpe, following early French reports that the pilot was David Henderson.

At 9am, Cardiff City's playing staff were told to take the day off as training was cancelled.

At 10.34am, Cardiff City chairman Mehmet Dalman said the club was "very worried" by reports and was contacting family members and emergency services to seek clarity. He continued, "We are very concerned by the latest news that a light aircraft lost contact over the Channel last night. We are awaiting confirmation

Emiliano Sala's last picture on board the fatal flight

before we can say anything further. We are very concerned for the safety of Emiliano Sala."

At 1.22pm, rescue workers conceded they were not expecting any survivors. John Fitzgerald, chief officer of the Channel Islands Air Search, announced: "I don't think the coastguard are either. We just don't know how it disappeared." He said the plane "just completely vanished. There was no radio conversation".

Back in Cardiff manager Neil Warnock got a call from Mark McKay informing him Sala had not shown up. The manager had already sent his squad home for the day as Ken Choo, Cardiff's chief executive, said the club was in deep distress, but they were praying for a miracle. "We were very shocked upon hearing the news that the plane had gone missing," said Choo, who had played a part in welcoming grieving Leicester City fans after the helicopter crash which had killed the Foxes' chairman Vichai Srivaddhanaprabha just three months earlier. "We expected Emiliano to arrive [on Monday] night into Cardiff and [Tuesday] was due to be his first day with the team. Our owner, Tan Sri Vincent Tan, and chairman, Mehmet Dalman, are very distressed about the situation. We made the decision first thing this morning to call off training with the thoughts of the squad, management staff and the entire club with Emiliano and the pilot."

Back in Nantes, the text that Sala promised to sent Pallois never arrived.

"Then everything happened so fast, it was so tough," Fabio later told Teesside Live. "I cannot explain." The Brazilian full-back, now a Nantes player, continued, "The next morning Nico said Sala hadn't texted and asked the club to call Cardiff to check he's alright. But Nico was OK at this stage, he was not worried because he thought Sala must have just forgotten. The guy who worked here called Cardiff and then we found out the plane hadn't arrived. As soon as he said that, everyone started to cry. When you say the plane is missing, we knew it was a big, big problem. That should have been the best moment of his life: that's what he'd been working for - a £15m move, playing Premier League football, his salary. That was the best time of his life. And that's what is the worst part for me to think about. He was such a fantastic guy, so brilliant to be around, a hard worker, first to arrive and last to leave. He was so happy. Everyone will say the same about him.

"I am a happy and positive guy anyway but this sort of thing, it makes you love the simple things. I came home that morning because we had no training, I came home and I hugged my two daughters and my wife like it was the last day of the world because you just never know. Hug your daughters, smile at them every day, smile at everyone you love every day, because you just never know, you never know."

Five aircraft and two lifeboats continued scouring more than 1,100sq miles of water and plane parts and seats had been spotted in the water but couldn't be positively identified as being from the missing plane.

On Friday, Sala had been posing alongside adoring Cardiff fans after putting pen to paper on his three-year deal, now the same six young men who had met the club's record signing returned to the ground to pay their respects leaving scarves and flowers. Oliver Watson, 17, from Barry, said. "We spotted Emiliano's car in the car park at the weekend. We saw him in the window of the stadium signing paperwork, so we hung around to try and meet him… he couldn't stop smiling. It was a brief encounter, but he asked how we were and that was really nice. When I saw the news, I just couldn't believe it. It was a shock. I can't believe it's happened. He hasn't even played a game for the club, but he signed for us which means he'll always be a part of the club. We'll never forget him!"

Nantes president Waldemar Kita said Sala was a "polite, nice, adorable boy, adored by everyone". He went on to say the whole club was praying for those on board, "I'm thinking of his friends, his family, I'm still in hope, he's a fighter, it's not over, maybe he's somewhere, waiting for some news that we hope will be positive, we are very touched by all the support received since this morning." The club, who play in yellow, called on supporters to join a vigil on Tuesday evening in the city to drop a yellow tulip at the foot of a fountain.

Sala's parents, Horatio and Mercedes, spoke to Argentine media after being informed of their son's plane disappearing. Horatio told Argentine TV station Channel 5 News "A friend told me, I did not know anything, I'm in Rosario, I'm working because I'm a truck driver. I just can't believe it. I'm desperate. I don't know what could have happened. I'm desperate, I hope everything goes well.

"To get the chance to play at a big European club was an amazing step for him and for his town back home. He is a humble small town boy. Everybody is watching the TV and waiting. Hopefully some good news arrives."

His mother, Mercedes, said she received a phone call from France to inform her about the tragic news. "They called me from France to tell me that his plane had gone missing and they were looking for him. The plane belongs to Cardiff City. We are in constant communication and desperate for good news. He was very happy and content with the transfer. He was enjoying the best moment of his career so far.

"Emiliano would come over often to visit us, and we would go to visit him there. He was alone, I didn't have any family members with him in France. We don't have any more news. The only thing I know is that the plane took off and they are searching for it, as we don't know anything yet, they haven't found anything. We are just here waiting, minute after minute. I spoke to him a few hours before he took off. I don't know what else to say, I'm so worried."

Sala's former club, Chamois Niortais FC, tweeted that the whole team was thinking of him as the search continued. "Tell us it's a joke... Emi.... All the Team Chamois thinking of you," tweeted the club's official account.

By midday on 22nd January the French Navy had joined in the search alongside the Channel Island Lifeboats and the UK Coastguard. The search was suspended as darkness fell and resumed at 8am on the 23rd but there was still no sign of debris as authorities examined satellite images and mobile data for clues to the plane's last known location.

On Thursday 24th January the search was officially abandoned as the Coastguard conceded that the chances of anyone surviving in those conditions were "extremely remote". The search had covered 1284 nautical square miles of the English Channel. Rescue crews had searched about 1,700 square miles of land and sea since the Piper PA-46 Malibu vanished from radar on Monday evening near the Channel Island of Alderney. Guernsey harbour-master Captain David Barker said it had been a "difficult" decision to call off the search, but explained the chances of survival were "extremely remote" given the time elapsed.

Captain Barker acknowledged the family were "not content" with the decision, but was "absolutely confident" no more could have been done. He insisted UK coastguard protocols were followed and hoped the families found some comfort in the incident remaining open, despite searches ceasing.

Three planes and five helicopters racked up 80 hours combined flying time looking for the plane, working alongside two lifeboats and other passing ships.

Emiliano Sala's sister, Romina, said she had held a meeting with investigators, but could not comment about it, and said the family were grateful for all the support they had received.

In a statement, Cardiff City said that it was "with a heavy heart" that the club learned of the decision to call off the search, while the Premier League said it was "deeply saddened", adding there would be silences before kick-offs at the next round of matches for "reflection" and as a mark of respect.

Cardiff City's owner Vincent Tan added, "Monday evening's news shook everyone at Cardiff City FC to the core. We also thank everyone involved with the search and rescue operation, and continue to pray for Emiliano, David Ibbotson and their families."

Chief executive Ken Choo praised Sala as a "humble man", adding: "He's willing to fight and join us [Cardiff City] and help us, so I view him as a hero." He said the club would provide information to the family, but added: "With a missing plane, there is a lot of information to acquire - it could take up to six months to a year."

Emiliano Sala's father Horacio spoke of their grief on TV as the official search was called off. "I cannot believe it ... this is a dream... a bad dream... I'm desperate," Horacio was speaking from his home in the town of Progreso when there was still no news on whether the remains of Sala or Ibbotson had been found in the wreckage.

His mother Mercedes and his sister Romina had flown to Guernsey as the search operation got underway. Romina said in an emotional social media message posted alongside a video collage featuring Sala on and off the pitch as a boy and a man, "Tell me this is a nightmare. Emi please return brother. Please. I love you so much."

Romina then travelled to Cardiff to hold a news conference, where she pleaded with authorities: "I beg them that they don't stop searching for them. Please, please, please don't stop the search. We understand the effort but please don't stop the search. We are convinced Emiliano and the pilot are alive somewhere in the channel."

Speaking through an interpreter, she added: "I'm still in shock. We know Emiliano and the pilot are still alive. We want to go and search for them. We're asking please don't stop with this effort. All together, we will find a way to restart the search to find Emiliano." Visibly emotional, she continued, "Emiliano is a great fighter - I know he hasn't given up and he is waiting for us. It is exasperating not to know where a relative is. At this moment all I think about is that the search continues. All I want is that him and the pilot are found."

Sala's ex-girlfriend Berenice Schkair urged presidents to "intervene". She said: "Emiliano Sala has to appear and be resolved through justice, we ask the presidents to intervene in the search!" In another emotional post on social media she added "I want to wake up and all of this to be a lie. Please investigate because I cannot believe this accident. I feel impotent, I'm in a nightmare. I cannot stop thinking about you, Emi." Schkair told Argentine media outlet 'Infobae' that she believed Emiliano was still alive "living on an island" and shed light on a previous tweet in which she had blamed a "football mafia" for the crash. She said: "It was an impulse. I sensed there was something strange, dark. But I don't have information about anything. The only thing I felt was if a plane disappears off the face of the Earth, two people disappear and nobody wants to search for them and everything stays covered then it is something strange."

Asked if she thought Emi's disappearance was an accident, she said "I want to think it was an accident but then I feel that there was a series of irresponsibilities which brought about this horror. The irresponsibility is a little bit on everyone's part. Why was the pilot there if he didn't have the correct licence? Why did the plane take off anyway despite Emi saying it was bad? Why did they send a plane in bad condition? Why did they take off in that weather? Why did the club not look after him if they had bought a player of that level?" When asked what she would do if Sala never showed up, she said: "Find the person responsible, they need to carry out an investigation and not leave everything covered up. If something that terrible happens, the family are going to have to fully investigate and knock on a lot of doors. But if Emi turns up the only thing that is going to matter to me is that he fulfils his dream and plays

David Ibbotson at the controls of the plane that crashed

football again."

Lionel Messi joined calls from across the global football community to continue the search, "While there is possibility, even a shred of hope, we ask don't stop searching." Writing on Instagram, the Argentina international megastar added: "All my strength and support to his family and friends."

Argentina's president joined calls for the search to resume. Mauricio Macri told his foreign minister to issue formal requests to Britain and France, according to a statement from his office. "President Mauricio Macri instructed foreign minister Jorge Faurie to make a formal request to the governments of Great Britain and France to ask them to maintain the search efforts." Mr Faurie made the request to both nations' embassies.

Manchester City's Argentine forward Sergio Agüero, used the social media hashtag #NoDejenDeBuscar translated as 'do not stop searching'. Agüero tweeted, "We don't want to give up, we want to hold on to hope... don't call off the search."

Agüero's City team-mate, Argentina defender Nicolas Otamendi, said on Twitter: "I'd like to express my sympathies to Emiliano's family, and urge the police to keep searching for the plane. There's still hope to find them alive. All my support to his family, and let's hope they get an answer urgently." Meanwhile Chelsea's new Argentine signing Gonzalo Higuain called on "the world" to use social media to ask that the search be continued. Newcastle United's Argentine defender Federico Fernandez, Marseille's France winger Florian Thauvin and Brazilian ex-Manchester United defender Fabio da Silva - now with Nantes - were among those to offer support to the search for Sala.

The reaction of the world's media focussed on the missing striker. "La disparition d'un guerrier," read the front page of *L'Equipe* which translantes as "The disappearance of a warrior." "I am so shaken," said former Caen teammate Felipe Saad. "He was a lovable, generous fellow. He always believed that football was a team sport. His move to Cardiff was going to bring him the recognition he deserved, albeit belatedly. He so deserved his talent to be recognised."

Alongside pleas from Nantes and prominent players for the search to continue, wreaths and tributes were laid by fans at Sala's clubs, including Cardiff, Nantes and San Martin de Progreso in Argentina. That Saturday was FA Cup 4th Round day for English clubs yet Millwall and Everton players did not wear black armbands during their televised tie on Saturday evening after Sala's family contacted the FA to ask them not to do so. Earlier in the day, black armbands had been worn as a mark of respect to the player. However, BBC commentator Jonathan Pearce confirmed during the tie at The Den that the family requested for the players not to wear them in the evening kick-off as he had not been confirmed dead. Pearce said, "The eagle-eyed among you may spot that the players are not wearing black armbands - in the earlier Cup ties today the players were wearing black armbands in respect to Emiliano Sala, the new Cardiff striker whose plane went down earlier this week. But his family contacted the FA earlier today and said they didn't want the black armbands because the player has not been confirmed dead yet. So that is why Millwall and Everton, out of respect to the family's wishes, are not wearing those armbands."

As a period of mourning for the missing player began, it was only a matter of time before there would be recriminations. Aside from the technicalities of the plane's disappearance, how had a player valued at £15m by Cardiff ended up on a single-engined plane piloted by a colour blind pilot who had no license to carry commercial passengers? The answer to that question would open up a Pandora's Box of blame between Cardiff, Nantes and agent Willie McKay.

Once the plane disappeared and the passenger was identified as Emiliano Sala, the assumption in the media was that the buying club had booked Sala's flight. Cardiff quickly issued a statement saying that the player had "made his own arrangements" to fly to Nantes and back which forced the player's agent, Willie McKay, to issue a statement a few days later admitting he had booked the fatal flight.

"I can confirm that when Emiliano made myself and his agent Meïssa N'Diaye aware that he wished to travel back to Nantes following his medical and signing on Friday, I began to look into arranging a private flight to take him to Nantes on Saturday morning" a statement read. "In regards to the booking of the flight, we contacted David Henderson who has flown us and many of our players all over Europe on countless occasions. We had no involvement in selecting a plane or a pilot and wish to make clear we do not own the plane that Emiliano flew on."

On the Friday evening it was confirmed a plane was available to fly Emiliano on Saturday which would remain in Nantes until he was due to return to Cardiff. McKay claimed not to know who owned the aircraft and stated categorically that it was not owned by him or any commercial entity linked to him. The Scot also claimed that Cardiff were aware of the travel arrangements.

A "moment of silent reflection" took place before the kick-offs in the next round of Premier League fixtures on the following Tuesday and Wednesday. Players sported black arm bands and took part in a moment of applause before their game as the Air Accidents Investigation Branch began an investigation scrutinising "all operational aspects," including licensing and flight plans. There were "alarm bells all around" the incident, aviation consultant Alastair Rosenchein told BBC Radio Wales' Good Morning programme. He said: "The one issue is whether a single-engine air craft should be flying at night, in winter, over water and with passengers. This is the real issue - it is a really bad combination." He said despite only 1,400 of this type of plane being built, there was a "quite significant" number of deaths and injuries from flights involving them.

Tributes were paid at Arsenal's Emirates stadium where Cardiff were playing in the game in which Sala should have made his Bluebird's debut. The falling rain epitomised the feeling of gloom and despondency during a subdued build up to the match, as there was still no trace of the missing Argentinian striker.

Neil Warnock described it as the worst moment in management. He even talked about quitting. Speaking for the first time since the disappearance of the plane, the 70-year-old manager revealed that his players had counselling in what he called "the most difficult week in my career by an absolute mile". Cardiff may have been returning to Premier League action at Arsenal but Warnock said his players' thoughts were elsewhere with the events of the last week affecting his team selection. "It's been a traumatic week and even now I can't get my head around the situation," Warnock said, "not very often have I ever said I am lost for words, but that's how I am at the moment. It's impossible to sleep. To be honest, I considered whether or not I wanted to carry on being a football manager last week. Even as I sit here now that would be the case because there are more important things. It takes something like this to make you realise that. It would be wrong to say everything is back to normal and I'm firing on all cylinders. It's not like that. My age isn't helping and it feels strange. You feel tired all the time, even when you have had a sleep, and the doctor says that is due to stress and it doesn't seem to get any easier at the moment." Warnock had sought help from the League Managers Association, and some players were "really poor in training" with a sombre mood hanging over the club.

Sala had met his new team-mates before heading back to Nantes. Central defender Sol Bamba said Cardiff's players regarded Sala as a team-mate and still held out hope that he was alive. After a week where players have been allowed to miss training if they did not feel ready to return to the pitch, they would wear daffodils to honour the Argentinian striker on their way to the Emirates Stadium. "We have had to go day by day to get over these traumatic events," Warnock said. Cardiff had hosted Leicester City back in November, the first game after the Foxes' owner Vichai Srivaddhanaprabha was killed in a helicopter crash when leaving the King Power Stadium. "The emotional effect the Leicester City game had on us, even though the loss wasn't about our club, made the game almost irrelevant," said Warnock. "We definitely couldn't have played on Saturday and now we've just got to get on with things. Whether Tuesday night will be good in that it puts something else in my mind I don't know. There has been a sombre mood all week, but it probably hit me harder than anyone else because I met Emiliano and had been talking to him for the last six or seven weeks.

"I called him Emile because I told him I probably wouldn't get his name right, and I told him he would fit in very well with my team because of the way he dressed. He had holes in his trousers and looked a bit scruffy. We've got a few like that. He said he would score goals for me and I told him I knew he would. I thought this was going to be a turning point for us, but now it's turned into a massive blow."

Cardiff were third from bottom in the table and Warnock admitted, "It was always a massive job for us in the first place to stay in the Premier League, now it is doubly massive. We would rather have Emiliano with us and get relegated than not have him. This is when you have to show your leadership and you have to show the lads you are in charge. We have to perform a miracle. You are the leader of the pack and you have to show leadership in the right areas. I think I am okay when I am in the public eye and with the players. My biggest problem is when I am on my own or at home with my wife Sharon and little things trigger it. It is amazing what keeps popping up."

Before the game daffodils were handed out as a gesture of support to Sala's proposed new home in South Wales. On each of the seats where the 2,000 Cardiff fans gathered was a giant yellow card. As the players came on to pitch, the cards were held up to form a giant yellow mosaic in the corner of the stadium. On the stadium the big screen showed a photo of Sala with the hashtag #prayforsala.

Amid the cards was an Argentinian flag with the name Emiliano Sala. Another scarf was held up with the name FC Nantes. Before kick-off, there was a round of applause. Warnock had wanted his players to show their professionalism and they responded with spirit and determination, and so too did an always animated manager. With his hood up against the elements Warnock was soon berating fourth official Kevin Friend as Cardiff were denied a penalty. The combative Harry Arter was booked, Bruno Manga mistimed a tackle on Sead Kolasinac and Pierre-Emerick Aubameyang scored from the spot. Alexandre Lacazette scored Arsenal's second. In stoppage time Nathaniel Mendea-Laing finished the night with a left-foot strike.

Cardiff received an invite from Nantes to attend their tribute game to Sala but it had arrived only two days before the match, and with insufficient time for the club to make the arrangements. Nantes paid tribute with gigantic murals of the Argentinian striker before their league game with St Etienne, their first game since Sala went missing. Sala's name was spelled out by supporters using yellow and green cards in the stands. Nantes fans laid flowers and football shirts outside of the Stade de la Beaujoire before kick-off while candles were lit nearby. As the home side warmed up, they donned white t-shirts with Sala's face on the front 'On t'aime Emi' – 'we love you Emi' – and wore green armbands symbolising hope during the match.

A video featuring his highlights as a Nantes player was played before the game at the Stade de la Beaujoire. Fans were visibly upset, and Argentina flags and 'Sala' scarves were waved in the stands. Each Nantes player had the missing striker's name on the back of their shirt during the match.

The emotional scenes moved Nantes manager Vahid Halilhodžic to tears during a minute's applause when the game was paused in the ninth minute as the whole stadium showed their appreciation.

The game ended in a 1-1 draw, both sides had a man sent off in first-half stoppage time, with Fabio and Yann M'Vila sent off for arguing with each other before Nantes's Waris Majeed cancelled out Remy Cabella's opener. Waris celebrating by tapping a photograph of Sala on a top under his shirt. FC Nantes tweeted images from inside the dressing room of Sala shirts.

There was bitterness from the Sala family and their frustrations manifested itself in an emotional outburst from Sala's father Horacio, who accused Cardiff City of 'abandoning' his son. Horacio died in April, just weeks after the interview in a BBC Wales documentary. He said "with all the money that had been paid for him, why was it so hard for them to find something safe? Why couldn't they? But they left him alone. They left him like a dog. They left him, they abandoned him."

Sala's mother, Mercedes Taffarel, who was also part of the documentary, added, "I keep thinking he's going to call, but no…"

*Emiliano Sala with his family; his brother Dario,
mother Mercedes and sister Romina*

*The McKay family: (left) Mark and his girlfriend Rachel Morse co-
owners of Mercato Sports; (top right) twins Jack and Paul, then on the
books at Cardiff City; (below) Willie McKay who was banned from
acting as a football agent in France.*

5: THE SEARCH RESUMES

THE OFFICIAL SEARCH FOR THE MISSING PLANE had been called off after just three days with Guernsey's harbour master announcing that the chances of survival for those on board was "extremely remote" but Emiliano Sala's family refused to give up hope, setting up a funding campaign which was backed by Lionel Messi and footballers from around the world including numerous Premier League stars including Laurent Koscielny, Ilkay Gundogan, and Sergio Agüero. The appeal quickly raised £324,000 to pay for a private search operation. More than 4,000 people immediately responded and the target was reached with the help of a £26,000 donation from French World Cup winner Kylian Mbappé. Other high-profile donors to the GoFundMe page included former West Ham midfielder Dimitri Payet and Leicester City winger Demarai Gray.

The fund had been set up by Sala's agent, the Paris-based sports agency Sport Cover. Meïssa N'Diaye worked with the French equivalent of the Professional Footballers' Association raise the funds. The initial target of 150,000 euros (£130,000) was met within 24 hours. In a message from the family published on the fundraising website, they said the tragedy went "far beyond football" and the money would be used "exclusively for research".

A petition signed by 41,462 people, said: "The clubs and their supporters are demanding that the search for Emiliano Sala and the pilot of the plane continue for their families and their loved ones." A message on the webpage carried the hashtag #NoDejenDeBuscar Emiliano Sala which translates as 'Don't Stop Looking for Emiliano Sala'. It said: "This fund was created in response to the urgency of the situation and the authorities' decision not to pursue the search. Its sole objective, through a specialised non-profit organisation, is to help the family of Emiliano and pilot Dave Ibbotson continue the search. Thank you for helping with the amount you want."

An American marine scientist known as the 'Shipwreck Hunter', David Mearns, promised he'd find answers but warned that the plane had "clearly broken up". Mearns volunteered to help the Sala family for free after initial search and rescue efforts by a number of agencies failed. Mearns focused his search on an area north of Guernsey. "I want to help them, as simple as that, any way we can," he said from Guernsey, "we are giving the families the best chance to find the answers they don't have. The family are devastated we're trying to provide answers, that's the ultimate objective. The plane has been badly broken up and we are looking for a debris field. We are confident of finding the wreckage in the next three days."

Emiliano's sister Romina travelled to Cardiff where she gave an emotional press conference before she arrived on Guernsey with her mother, Mercedes. "This is a family that has come from Argentina with this huge shock out of nowhere and is struggling with very, very few answers about an unexplained loss" Mearns added. He said that the family "still have some hope", saying, "They're looking at this as a missing person, a missing plane and until they are satisfied that's the mode that we are in."

The family were taken to see the area, circling the island of Alderney. Family and friends arrived in Guernsey and several members of the group were later taken to the small island of Burhou. The islet was the focus of social media attention on the night of the disappearance after members of the public shared a picture which appeared to show flares coming from the island. However John Fitzgerald, the director of Channel Islands Air Search, said the island and its surrounding area had been searched many times. He added, "It is really a puffin reserve. It is tiny but you can land on it. The plane and helicopters have been over it many times since [the night the plane vanished], but they haven't seen anything in that area. It is only a few hundred metres long and it has been saturated by helicopters and fixed-wing aircraft. The flares I have seen pictures of are most likely aircraft trails."

There were two vessels at Mearns disposal and the salvage

expert said he would divide the search area in half, looking for wreckage and a debris field to a depth of 60-120m (196-390ft). "We will continue to work until the plane is located," he said. "More investigative technical searches underwater would be undertaken at some point," he continued . He said the family thanked donors for their "exceptional generosity".

Mearns, who claimed to have found 24 major shipwrecks, led the search. He said that the boat, called Morven, had been brought from Southampton to Guernsey six hours earlier than scheduled to take advantage of a break in the weather. The two boats hired using the crowd funded money resumed the search. The boat, operated by global marine cable installation firm A-2-Sea, was equipped with the latest technology, including a multi-beam echosounder and side-scan sonar, which can detect anomalies on the seabed.

Mearns said Guernsey authorities were answering all the family's questions about their investigations. "But as you know locally the search was terminated on Thursday and that was what triggered this private search. Today, even as an expert, my frame of thinking is alongside with the family's, that's what I'm trying to do. But we're trying to give them the best advice we possibly can. You have to appreciate they don't know the environment, they don't know the geography."

The AAIB carried out a search from the vessel Geo Ocean III, which had left Ostend in Belgium at 9am and began combing the area. Within hours the FPV Morven picked up a sonar signal from the depths. The AAIB said its search was expected to last three days, while the private search would continue "until the plane is located". Mearns said his team on board the FPV Morven would work jointly with the AAIB's vessel. They planned to search an area covering four square miles about 24 nautical miles north of Guernsey. The location was selected because it was on the flight path of the plane before it lost radar contact.

Once the specialist search began off the coast of Guernsey the wreckage was located on the seabed within hours. The crowd-funded vessel picked up sonar signal and wreckage was probed for clues as to what happened, but that was hardly likely to be fruitful in such inaccessible circumstances. The wreckage of the Piper Malibu was formally identified by officials from the Air Accident Investigation Board. The AAIB's vessel deployed a remote-controlled submarine to examine the plane and that night confirmed it was the craft carrying the striker.

Mearns said the discovery had been so quick because the team had been looking for a static object rather than in a dynamic environment searching for survivors. The sea search vessel FPV Morven detected the wreckage using sonar and an unmanned Air Accident Investigation Branch submarine sent to the sea bed used an HD camera to identify the blue and white aircraft.

Now it was imperative to salvage the plane wreck to look for clues as to the plane's demise. Mearns, who had spearheaded around 20 historic wreck recoveries, including one of Britain's most famous battleships the HMS Hood, said with the right equipment it should be a relatively straightforward job to lift the plane. He said it would need to be done in "slack water" – the point at which the tide is turning. Mearns said a salvage vessel equipped for working in the North Sea and a properly equipped dive support vessel would be able to lift the vessel within a matter of days.

On Thursday 7th February, three days after the wreckage had been found, a body was discovered. When asked if it would be recovered before the wreck itself, Mearns said, "That's down to the AAIB and their operational people about how they do that. The body will be the most sensitive of objects that they are picking up so they will be very careful about that – they will undoubtedly have people on board who are experienced with the recovery of human remains. Sadly this is not the first time this will have happened. I'm sure they will have the right professionals out there for that."

Mearns stayed in regular contact with the Sala family by text message because of the language barrier. "We are informing them every step of the way what's going on and they are making it clear to us what their priorities are at all times. There's a much greater chance they will get answers if (the plane is) recovered. I haven't spoken to them, but they were devastated the last time we were here and frankly the news is worse today. Now their worst fears are confirmed, so I would imagine they would be just as devastated – it's going to take a long time for them to come to terms with the loss."

The discovery came just two days after cushions from a plane were found on a beach near Surtainville on France's Cotentin Peninsula in Normandy, France, directly east of Guernsey where the plane disappeared from radar. The AAIB said a body had been recovered and taken to Portland to be passed over to the Dorset coroner for examination.

The aircraft remained 67 metres underwater 21 miles off the coast of Guernsey. The AAIB said attempts to recover the aircraft wreckage were unsuccessful due to continued poor weather, "the difficult decision was taken to bring the overall operation to a close". The Geo Ocean III search boat returned to dock in Portland, Dorset, carrying some wreckage of the Piper Malibu aircraft.

Families of both men were informed of the discovery. Sala's father said he had not had any contact with the rest of his family – who were still in a hotel in Nantes – and found out about the plane's discovery on TV. "I communicated with them every day, but since I do not have Whatsapp it's hard to call them or call me. They told me that the days passed and there was no news of Emiliano or the plane," said Horacio. He said that the family were in the hotel along with 'eight or nine' friends who received the news from Argentine embassies in France and England, at 9am.

Mearns called the news 'devastating' but told Sky News that "at least we were able to bring some sort of answer to the families'"

Shipwreck hunter David Mearns tweets the news that the families had been dreading

Mearns added, "but tonight they have heard devastating news and in respect of the families I won't comment any further about what has happened."

Police confirmed that the body found in the plane wreckage was that of Sala after an unidentified body – now known to be Sala – was brought off the ship Geo Ocean III on a stretcher and transferred to a private ambulance before being taken to Dorset Police and the local coroner.

Finally, a statement from Dorset Police, released on Thursday night, read, "The body brought to Portland Port today, Thursday 7th February 2019, has been formally identified by HM Coroner for Dorset as that of professional footballer Emiliano Sala. The families of Mr Sala and the pilot David Ibbotson have been updated with this news and will continue to be supported by specially-trained family liaison officers. Our thoughts remain with them at this difficult time. HM Coroner will continue to investigate the circumstances of this death supported by Dorset Police.

"On Monday 21 January 2019 a plane carrying both men was flying from Nantes to Cardiff when it lost contact with Air Traffic Control, north of Guernsey. Sadly a search and rescue operation was unsuccessful in locating the plane and the two occupants. Subsequently AAIB and privately funded search teams were deployed to the relevant area. Using specialist equipment the teams succeeded in locating and identifying the plane and recovering Mr Sala's body."

The body was recovered from the aircraft wreckage using ROVs (remotely-operated vehicles) to pull it from the water in "as dignified a way as possible". The red and white vessel carrying the body docked at Portland, Dorset, at around 9:15. The boat was met at the harbour by two police cars, including a 4x4, with a silver coroner's van arriving at the scene at around 9:45am. Several of the ship's crew could be seen leaving the 25ft vessel to introduce themselves to authorities before showing police and the coroner on board.

The Piper Malibu aircraft remained more than 200 feet below water and was 21 miles off the coast of Guernsey in the English

Balotelli et Marseille, le mariage de raison

L'ÉQUIPE

EMILIANO SALA
LA DISPARITION D'UN GUERRIER

FC Nantes

@FCNantes

Jan 24

Le FC Nantes a appris l'abandon des recherches de l'avion disparu.

Celles-ci ne peuvent s'arrêter. Le Club et ses supporters demandent avec force que les recherches pour retrouver @EmilianoSala1 continuent, pour sa famille et pour ses proches.

Ensemble, pour Emi !

#PrayForSala

Florian Thauvin ✓
@FlorianThauvin

Follow

Pour Sala, pour sa famille et ses proches les recherches ne peuvent pas s'arrêter ! Il faut encourager la police à continuer les recherches ! Sala est un guerrier, il faut croire en lui ! #PrayforSala @GuernseyPolice

Translate Tweet

6:11 PM - 24 Jan 2019

Fabio Da Silva ✓
@Ofabio9

Follow

#prayforsala 🙏 please @GuernseyPolice

Valentin Rongier ✓ @Valrongier28
La recherche ne peut pas s'arrêter! Aidez nous a encourager la police à continuer les recherches. On a besoin de tout le monde. Battons nous comme Émi le fait tout le temps s'il vous plaît. #PrayforSala @GuernseyPolice

6:42 PM - 24 Jan 2019

Sergio Kun Aguero ✓
@aguerosergiokun

Follow

We don't want to give up, we want to hold on to hope. That's why I also wish #NoDejenDeBuscar - don't call off the search. From the start, my thoughts have been with Emiliano, his family and friends #PrayForSala

10:28 PM - 24 Jan 2019

GARDONS ESPOIR

SALA 9

Tributes poured in for Sala from the world of football

Channel for more than two weeks as poor weather conditions stopped efforts to recover it. While one body was successfully brought to the surface, poor conditions saw the decision made that crews would be unable to bring the wreckage itself to land. The Air Accidents Investigation Branch added, "Following extensive visual examination of the accident site using the remotely operated vehicle (ROV), it was decided to attempt recovery operations. In challenging conditions, the AAIB and its specialist contractors successfully recovered the body previously seen amidst the wreckage. The operation was carried out in as dignified a way as possible and the families were kept informed of progress.

"Unfortunately, attempts to recover the aircraft wreckage were unsuccessful before poor weather conditions forced us to return the ROV to the ship. The weather forecast is poor for the foreseeable future and so the difficult decision was taken to bring the overall operation to a close. The body is currently being taken to Portland to be passed into the care of the Dorset Coroner. Although it was not possible to recover the aircraft, the extensive video record captured by the ROV is expected to provide valuable evidence for our safety investigation."

Sala's sister Romina posted a photo on her Instagram along with a heartfelt tribute to him. The footballer's loyal dog was pictured waiting for his owner to come home; a photo showed the black Labrador staring out into the street after the plane carrying him between Nantes and the Welsh capital crashed into the sea. The dog was one of the reasons for Sala's return to France as the striker also said farewell to his former teammates. He took his beloved pet to kennels before starting the process of moving her to the UK to live with him.

Romina referred her brother's 'faithful companion', tweeting a photo of Sala and the dog, and another with the message: 'Naja, your faithful companionship is now ours. (We never thought of giving her up for adoption. I will clarify this to ensure people are aware).' Sala's ex-girlfriend, Berenice Schkair, posted a picture on Instagram of a rose stuck into the sand next to the sea.

David Ibbotson's daughter, sister and nephew were among loved ones paying their respects. His younger sister Helen Kapatysulias wrote, "To David, my gentle brother. I have so many memories of you, mine is of you when you were coming home from school, you used to pick me up and carry me home. I will lock these memories in my heart forever. All I would like is to see your face, smiling, cheekily, again. I know you're safe wherever you are. I pray that one day I will see you again, my gentle Big Brother. I love you forever and always and will never forget you."

His daughter penned "In loving memory of a dear Dad: 'Daddio, words cannot describe how much I am going to miss you. You are the best dad anybody could wish for and I will love you always. I have (word illegible) memories and will pass these on to anybody I meet. All my love Vicki."

In another tribute among dozens laid around a tree in the market square in his home village of Crowle, near Scunthorpe, North Lincolnshire, his nephew Tim wrote, "To my uncle David. We hope that the angels are looking and guiding you home to us. I love you lots."

Tributes quickly poured in for Emiliano Sala on social media. Diego Maradona, who was among those who had called on authorities not to give up trying to find the footballer, paid tribute on Instagram. Alongside a picture of a match-day programme featuring Sala, saying, "I am very sorry for this sad news. Many of us kept a light of hope for you, Emiliano. I send a big hug to your family and friends."

Arsenal midfielder Mesut Özil added, "No words to describe how sad this is. Thoughts and prayers go out to his family and also to the family of the pilot." Liverpool defender Dejan Lovren posted a heartfelt message on Instagram saying, "I prayed every day because hope is the last. This is a great deal to accept. I can not even imagine how difficult it is for you [Sala's family]. We are all with you!" Fellow Argentine, Sergio Agüero, said, "Terribly sad. Rest in peace, Emiliano. My condolences to his friends and family." Wayne Rooney tweeted a black and white picture of Sala with the message: "Rest in peace. Thoughts are with friends and family" while Chelsea defender Antonio Rudiger added, "Heartbreaking to hear the news about Emiliano Sala. Rest in peace! Thoughts go out to the family and friends of Emiliano and the pilot."Kylian Mbappé, Antonio Valencia and Ruben Loftus-Cheek all posted tributes on social media in tribute to Sala.

Cardiff released a statement on their website which read, "We offer our most heartfelt sympathies and condolences to the family of Emiliano. He and David will forever remain in our thoughts."

Nantes retired their No 9 shirt in honour of Sala and in tearful scenes outside the club's Stade de la Beaujoire a 'keep hope' banner was removed in front of the floral tribute. The French club released a heartfelt statement confirming the decision to retire the shirt. "FC Nantes had the immense sadness on Thursday to learn that the body found was that of Emiliano Sala. This news puts an end to interminable and unbearable waiting. Emiliano will forever be on the legends who has written the great history of FC Nantes. There are difficult mornings, nightmarish awakenings, where unhappily reality hits us. Emis is gone...

"Emiliano Sala arrived on the banks of the Erdre in July 2015 and knew how to win the hearts of the Nantes supporters. With his work, his desire and his kindness without limits, he finished as the club's top scorer in his three seasons. The homages paid to him nationally and internationally match the player and person that he was. Today, we have lost a friend, a talented player and an exemplary team-mate. We can't forget in this drama the pilot and his family and have confidence that the authorities will continue their search."

Waldemar Kita, president of Nantes added, "I don't have the words. It's a tragedy, I'm crushed. Emiliano left his mark. That's why, like many fans, I wish to honour him by retiring the No 9. Nantes, its board, its staff and its players, wish to pass the families of Emiliano Sala and David Ibbotson their deepest condolences. We will never forget you, Emi. He's an Argentine who never gives up, Emiliano Sala, Emiliano Sala..."

Nantes paid a special tribute in their clash with Nîmes, the team wearing black shirts bearing the Argentine's name and all tickets to the game cost 9 Euros in reference to the forward's number.

Nantes manager Vahid Halilhodžic vowed to create a 'sacred union' amongst his squad.

Halilhodžic looked gaunt as he addressed the media ahead of his side's Ligue 1 game. "We always kept hope," he said, "knowing full well that it was almost an illusion. The truth has fallen - terrible, unfair. The situation is a little different for families. But it's terrible. We can now pay tribute to someone who will leave an eternal mark on this club, with his behaviour, his modesty."

With the clash with Nîmes the start of a run of three matches in seven days, Halilhodžic struggled to pick up his players. "These are essential matches in our position," added Halilhodžic, whose side were six points above the relegation zone, "I do not know how we will get out of it, but I will try to create this sacred union. The group must come out with character to get by. Today's terrible news gives us a terrible shock at a crucial moment. We need results now. Whether it's the players or the staff, everyone must make the effort to work and play together. I do what I can do, but I need everyone right now. It takes a lot of character to play a Ligue 1 match right now. I hope we will come out stronger."

Nantes were fined a combined £18,250 after supporters set off flares during matches as part of a tribute. Ligue 1's disciplinary commission had already fined the club £14,300 after supporters set off flares and threw objects in a league match against Saint-Étienne on 30 January, the club's first game after the Argentinian's disappearance. They were also fined £4,000 for a similar tribute by fans in their league game against Nîmes.

Before their next game at Caen, a series of tributes were planned by the home club for whom Sala had played just a few seasons earlier. Caen paid tribute to the Argentinian in an open letter published on their website, "Emi, it is hard to say goodbye to you so we start by saying 'thank you'. Wherever you are watching us from, we will try to provide the most beautiful spectacle. We will share in the pain of your Nantes team-mates - our opponents are your friends. We know that for you football was a way of life so we will do all we can to pay tribute to you, to take inspiration from you."

Players warmed up in T-shirts bearing the slogan 'Play for Sala', while Caen's playing shirts carried his name with a minute's applause for the 14th minute, in honour of Sala's shirt number in his time with the club. There was a pre-match video and tribute programme dedicated to him. Nantes earned a 1-0 win at Caen which lifted them away from trouble near the foot of the table. Nantes were reduced to 10 men in the 35th minute when Andrei Girotto saw red for his second bookable offence in the space of nine minutes. They snatched victory through Valentin Rogier's 81st-minute penalty after Alexander Djiku fouled Majeed Waris. The win lifted Nantes up to 14th place, eight points clear of the bottom three. Claudio Ranieri, Sala's former manager at Nantes, commented, "Emiliano was a player who put his head where others do not dare to put their feet."

On February 5th, just 14 days after the crash and with Emiliano Sala's body yet to be found, FC Nantes issued a demand to FIFA over Cardiff City's refusal to pay the first instalment of the £15m transfer fee. The French club had set the wheels in motion in a row that was going to last for months, if not years! "We can confirm that we have received yesterday evening a claim from FC Nantes against Cardiff City in connection with the transfer of Emiliano Sala," a FIFA spokesperson said, "we are looking into the matter and consequently we have no further comments at this stage." Cardiff insisted the Air Accidents Investigation Branch (AAIB) had to release its full findings first which could take years.

The Welsh side had been due to make the first of three instalments on 20th February but agreed with Nantes to extend the deadline by a week. Cardiff were withholding payment until crash investigations were complete and they were satisfied about "anomalies" around the deal. Nantes decision to force the issue had major repercussions because it arrived before Sala's body had been recovered from the sea and funeral arrangements had not yet

FC Nantes ✓
@FCNantes

Tous Sala.

#FCNASSE | #PlayForSala

Tributes poured in for Sala including messages from his sister Romina who published a picture of the striker with his beloved dog, Nala.

© Instagram - Romina Sala

salaromina • Follow

salaromina Your soul in my soul
will shine forever.
thus illuminating the time of my existence.
I love you. tito.

Load more comments

by_olliver My condolences to your
entire family from Laguna Paiva, near
the town of Emi. We spent joy reading
El Litoral the happy news of his pass
for being a player in our area. to the
uncertainty. that early morning. of the
terrible event ... The hopes of people
like me. unknown to you. remained
intact. today. .. I send you a big hug
😢

zubby_786 RIP Emiliano Sala 😢 such
a tragic sad story . Praise to all the
people involved in raising the money
which has helped not only find him.

♡ ○ ⎘

8,535 likes
15 MINUTES AGO

Add a comment...   ...

been finalised.

Chairman Mehmet Dalman confirmed Nantes' request in an interview with *L'Equipe*, "The only thing I can say because it is a sensitive subject is that I confirm that what you are saying is true. And to be honest, I do not want to say anything more. The first thing is that the body has not been recovered yet. We must show respect to the family. There is the process of recovering the plane. It's too early for us to comment. When we think it's the right time to do it (we will comment). I do not think the Cardiff club said it was not going to pay."

Sala's former club Girondins de Bordeaux quickly issued a public denial that they had invoiced Nantes for their cut of the deal as they were embarrassed by the timing of Nantes' demand – they were due a 50% sell on fee. A second demand in the space of a week was then emailed from Nantes to Cardiff, insisting they are paid. The French club threatened legal action if they did not receive a payment within 10 days, but that deadline came and went, and Nantes had yet to begin any legal action.

The Welsh club were taken aback by the timing of the correspondence as underwater rescue teams were in still in the process of attempting to retrieve the plane. James Hotson, a spokesman for the AAIB, said: "We can't give an indication at the moment of when the plane will be raised and we haven't given an indication that we are going to raise it."

Sala's mother, sister and brother were still with the Argentine consul in France after a body was located in the aircraft but the families of both pilot and player had still yet to be informed of the identity. There was understandable disgust by the Sala family that financial discussions were already taking place while the search for continued.

Cardiff later released a statement of their own which insisted that the authorities must be allowed to complete their investigation. It read: "Cardiff remain committed to ensuring fairness and accountability with respect to the agreement, but first and foremost the relevant authorities must be allowed to determine the facts surrounding this tragedy. It is inappropriate to comment further at this stage."

Cardiff suspected that Nantes were under extreme pressure because of ancillary payments to the agents and Sala's former club Bordeaux. Cardiff suspected there might even be monies owed to third parties in South America, although there was no evidence to support this.

Later Willie McKay claimed during a BBC TV interview that he was not pushing for his substantial cut insisting, "I don't care, to tell the truth – I really don't care because what we've been through is total hell." Cardiff thought otherwise as McKay was in constant communication with the club. Sources described unpleasant calls as the Scot chased his money.

As early as the week of the crash, a *Telegraph* investigation had discovered that Cardiff's case was based around one simple fact – "Who did the player belong to when he stepped onto the plane? And who was liable for the tragedy?" The Welsh club's stance was that the contract Sala signed when he was photographed at the club celebrating his 'signing' had been returned by the Premier League as invalid because it broke their regulations regarding players contracts, and so, technically, when Sala began his doomed flight, negotiations were still on-going to resolve the contract. In addition, Cardiff's negligence claim was spelled out as another significant reason to suspend the scheduled payments to Nantes until all the issues were resolved.

EXCLUSIVE: Cardiff consider legal action over the Emiliano Sala plane disaster as they face £14m loss

Tom Morgan, sports news correspondent, Harry Harris and Jamie Johnson, in Guernsey

25 JANUARY 2019

Cardiff City could launch a negligence claim over the Emiliano Sala plane disaster as the club faces a financial loss of around £14 million even after insurance payouts, The *Daily Telegraph* can disclose.

Senior figures at the club are increasingly concerned by the decision to fly their record signing across the English Channel in a single-engined plane built in 1984 and piloted by a part-time gas engineer.

Cardiff are now considering their legal position as they face a three-year contract bill estimated by accountants at £30million. Accident insurance is only likely to cover half the forecasted loss. One source said payments from Cardiff to Nantes have been frozen until officials have established the facts from the crash.

The club told The *Telegraph*: "Cardiff has made its position very clear that it had nothing to do with the arrangements of the flight, and now new information is coming in every day as we are continuing to investigate the chain of events and the cause of the accident. We are looking at the potential possibility of negligence that may have caused the accident."

The flight was booked independently by Sala's agent and Mark McKay, an intermediary in the deal. Emergency services believe the plane crashed into the sea on Monday night after taking off from Nantes, north-west France. The club is particularly keen to discuss the chain of events with the owners of the US-registered Piper PA-46-310P Malibu.

A total £20million transfer fee had been agreed with Nantes, including a £3million bonus if the club survived relegation. Sala had been due at his first training session in Wales on Tuesday. The transfer documents had already been filed with the Football Association and FIFA. Cardiff "will pay whatever is due, once they have established all the answers and can determine all the facts", a source said.

The search for the aircraft officially ended on Thursday, against the wishes of Sala's family. Rescue crews had covered an area of around 1,700 square miles of land and sea without finding any remains of the aircraft. Yesterday, Lionel Messi and Diego Maradona both supported calls to resume the search. A receptionist at the hotel where the pilot had been staying also added to the mystery by saying she believed the plane had been due to leave up to 10 hours before it eventually took off.

The club is believed to have had £16million (20.9m euros) of personal accident (PA) protection with the financial giant Lloyd's to cover its players. Trade magazine *Insurance Insider* reports the club's accident policy is led by China Re Syndicate 2088 and brokered by Miller. Sala's name is likely to have been added to the Premier League club's policy when the transfer was completed on January 19, just two days before his death. China Re's lead line represents around 16 percent of the total limit, with other Lloyd's insurers set to pay the rest of the claim. The Piper Malibu aircraft, which vanished off the coast of Guernsey, is also insured in the London market.

The minimum £17million transfer fee for the Argentinian striker, excluding the £3million Premier League survival bonus. was previously agreed to be paid in three instalments. The player's agent, Meïssa N'Diaye, and McKay were also due huge windfalls.

In addition to the £30million bill - which includes Sala's projected salary and fees - the club is braced for a subsequent impact on revenue from sponsorship arrangements and shirt sales. One source said the club will pay Nantes "whatever they believe to be a fair amount once they have established all the possibilities, including any negligence claims".

The plane was built in 1984, and was registered in the United States rather than Britain through a company based in Norfolk. The owners said in a statement issued by Southern Aircraft Consultancy they are "fully cooperating with the appropriate authorities, including the AAIB (air investigators) and police".

The pilot, Dave Ibbotson, held a private pilot's licence, according to US Federal Aviation Administration records. There is no public record of him having a commercial qualification. Ian Marshall, a friend of Mr Ibbotson's who sat with him on the British Parachute Association council, told *The Guardian* "Most of the pilots who have these private licences are semi-commercial. You're not meant to fly for any financial reward but that's not to say you can't fly for reasonable expenses. That's how many of them get around it."

Ken Choo, the Cardiff chief executive, recognised the club is now facing a severe striker shortage as the transfer window expires. However, the interim Premier League chief executive Richard Masters has apparently told him the league is powerless to offer any special dispensations to make a signing beyond the end of January.

Back in Wales, it emerged that some players turned down joining Cardiff on transfer deadline day because of the Sala tragedy. Neil Warnock had signed Leandro Bacuna from Reading for £3m, but failed in attempts to sign a striker. "One or two of the strikers we were talking about didn't really want to come in the circumstances," he said, "they didn't want to come in after what's happened. So it's been a very difficult window." Cardiff's only other deadline-day signing was Haverfordwest forward Danny Williams, who joined the club's under-23 squad. Warnock also said that attempts to bolster his squad were thwarted by the 'astronomical' figures that he had been quoted for players. "Overall, that's probably as good a window as we expected with the targets we achieved and the circumstances. We could probably have done with another one but we weren't going to have a gun put to our heads. For one lad abroad we were looking at, and the sort of finances we were talking about, you'd have thought he had been playing for his country on a regular basis. When they start talking the sort of money I paid for Bacuna for a signing-on fee and an agent's fee, I don't think we're into that. I wouldn't jeopardise the club or the owners by condoning that, so we had to pull a plug on a couple of deals. One of the deals was possibly close, but it was astronomical in the end. Things seemed to change every day. Whether they were pushing on our circumstances, I don't know, but we pulled out."

Cardiff City had a requested to conduct transfer dealings after the window closed on 31st January rejected. The club had asked the Premier League for "special dispensation". Chief executive Ken Choo said the request was "not something the Premier League could consider". He added the decision was something the club understands and had been anticipating.

Neil Warnock abandoned plans for Cardiff to take a mid-season break so that he and his players could reflect in private with their families. The Bluebirds had outplayed Bournemouth to lift Warnock's side to within two points of safety. When Bobby Reid converted an early penalty Cardiff's team, led by captain Sol Bamba, raced to the dugout and unveiled a blue T-shirt featuring a print of Sala's face. 'Emiliano, our beautiful bluebird,' read the match day programme, dedicating eight pages to the striker. Supporters wore daffodils while a mosaic appeared behind the goal, as Sala's name was emblazoned in yellow letters on the blue and white of the Argentine flag. As players bowed heads for the minute silence on the centre circle, advertising hoardings read, "For Emiliano, for David". A picture appeared of Sala on the big screens at both ends.

Afterwards Warnock said, "The crowd were amazing all the way round. It's been a very emotional 10 days. It got to me in the end, it can't be helped can it? It's one of those things. The players were amazing – I thought they were at Arsenal as well. I was disappointed we didn't win the other night. Today it was just not about surviving, I thought we played well as well, because they're a decent team." Warnock was also proud of how the club had handled the situation and believed Sala would feel the same, "I thought the attitude was fabulous today. We played some good stuff and we broke well. And the crowd, I can't believe it. I said to the lads that he's not here today but Emiliano would be proud of us all. I thought as a football club we acted amazing. I'm pleased for the chairman and Ken Choo. It's great for all of us and now we can get on with the rest of the season. We've told the other teams now that we won't give up without a fight. We can't have much more in my career. To have the Leicester City thing in the first game here and then this on top. I've known the lad for a couple of months so you get attached to them. I'm proud to be the Cardiff manager, that's for sure."

Bamba praised how the team handled the difficult situation, "Credit to the lads, it's been a difficult couple of weeks" while goalscorer Reid added "The lads have had a tough few weeks. It was right [to hold up a shirt with his name on] for him and his family."

The following Saturday saw another crucial 2-1 victory at Southampton but Cardiff would not play again until they hosted Watford on February 22 and although Warnock had planned to take his squad to Tenerife ahead of the run-in that would determine their Premier League status, following the events of the past few weeks he believed players would benefit from time with their families while some of the players had become fearful of flying since the incident. "The club gave me permission to fly out to Tenerife, to take them all for four days, but after what's happened over the past two weeks, I'd rather cuddle my kids and see my missus. I've never known anything like this in my life and I've seen most things. They'll all be reflecting on what's happened and your family is more important than football, isn't it? Some are booking different flights and some of them aren't going anywhere. I'm going somewhere near Swansea for two nights. Victor Camarasa's going back to Spain for a few days, that'll be good, he'll be having treatment on his calf and he'll be training with his fitness guy over there and in nicer weather with his family."

There was a minute's silence at St Mary's while Cardiff fans wore daffodils in memory of the Argentine. They also sang his name throughout. Sol Bamba, who scored Cardiff's other goal, said afterwards, "it's been a tough couple of weeks. I know Emiliano Sala was looking from up there so it's good to get the three points." Victory was secured by goals from Bamba and Kenneth Zohore either side of Jack Stephens' late equaliser which meant that for the first time since April 1962 the club had won successive top-flight fixtures – which was amazing considering the fortnight they had to endure. To take three points against a side unbeaten in the Premier League in 2019 was remarkable. "Looking at the bookies this morning, we were 4/1 in a two-horse race and no one expected us to win," Warnock said, "we were determined. While we're limited, you cannot question the character or what my players have got under their shirts. We wanted to do it for Emiliano and I'm really proud the lads have done him justice. One of my staff said the point might have kept us up. I think when you get to my age you don't worry too much really. You don't know what's around the corner, especially what's happened around here the last two weeks.'

Midfielder Aron Gunnarsson added, "Sala's death has brought everyone together, the performances and the fans and the lads and everyone around the club have been amazing at this difficult time. It has been really difficult but the boys have stuck together with everyone around the club. The most important thing was for the family to mourn. Knowing that now, hopefully, the pilot will be found and his family can mourn. It has been difficult but we have stuck together and our gaffer said after the game. This one was for Sala."

Players in games across the Premier League and EFL wore black armbands in tribute to Sala. A minute's silence was held at all Champions League and Europa League games as well that week. "On behalf of everyone at UEFA, I would like to express my sincerest condolences to the family and loved ones of Emiliano Sala for their loss," UEFA president Aleksander Ceferin said in a statement on the governing body's website. "I am deeply saddened that his life was so cruelly taken away at such a young age and I urge supporters across the continent to pay their respects to his memory over the coming days." UEFA confirmed clubs had the option of wearing black armbands.

With special tributes planned, Warnock added, "Whatever the families want or think, we'll adhere to that. We have had to get back to playing. And once we get this weekend out the way and we can move on, we have to regroup. We have to come up with a formula to get points on the board. People will write us off and quite rightly so. Other clubs have players like (Solomon) Rondon and (Aleksander) Mitrovic, doing what they are doing, but we don't have one of them. So it is more difficult for us, we have to make our own luck now and really have a go."

The football family wasn't completely united however as two

Southampton fans were detained by police for mocking Sala's death by making airplane gestures towards Cardiff City supporters inside St Mary's Stadium. Sickening footage emerged showing two men in the stands at St Mary's stretching their arms out wide and pretending to be planes towards the away end. Cardiff fans can be heard in the video calling them 'sick' while a steward approached the pair. Both fans had their details taken by Hampshire Police and faced three-year banning orders from the South Coast club. A Southampton statement read, "Southampton Football Club can confirm that two fans were detained and had their details taken by police during our match against Cardiff City on Saturday. The club will continue to work with Hampshire Police to identify any individuals deemed to have made indecent gestures towards Cardiff supporters. Such behaviour has no place in our game and will not be tolerated at St Mary's. The club will be taking an extremely firm stance against anyone involved and intends to ban those supporters identified."

EMILIANO SALA'S FUNERAL was a mixture of grief and fury in the small Argentinian town of Progreso where the player grew up. Emi's grieving cousin Martin Gatti showed his fury after he paid his last respects; he spoke to the press alongside another cousin and an aunt after the wake saying "It was an avoidable tragedy. This is a very personal point of view but there were a lot of irregularities that I'm sure the courts will have to investigate. It can't just end up like this, with the plane crashing and it being written off as a simple accident with the deaths of two people and nothing more than that. They have to start looking into this from the very beginning, from scratch, from point zero, from when they signed the contract, who put him on that plane, who organised the plane, who hired the pilot and why he was sent alone and without his representatives. Did any of his representatives come to his funeral? No."

Asked for his opinion by a local TV station Gatti added, "For

The family of Emiliano Sala arrived in France and were kept abreast of the search (top left). (Top right) The pilot David Ibbotson and his wife Nora, (left) a plane similar to the one which crashed.

A spectacular tribute to Emiliano Sala at Nantes home game with St. Etienne me Emiliano was killed. There were a lot of vested interests, and when there's a lot of money involved there are people who don't care about the lives of others." Gatti insisted Sala's family shared his view that his cousin had not received proper care. "The plane crashed at night and in bad weather conditions and he was alone. It's a very personal feeling but Emi's family feel the same way I do. I've spoken to his gran and his father. Everything was done wrong. That poor lad wasn't protected properly. It was all very irregular. For me this wasn't an accident. There were irregularities that caused an accident."

Many in Argentina seemed to suspect some kind of conspiracy with Berenice Schkair, the Argentinian model who had been romantically linked to the striker, pinning the "football mafia" tweet she had published and then taken down on the night the light aircraft disappeared.

Cardiff were well represented at the funeral. Vincent Tan told Sala's relatives he would pay a £50,000 personal donation for the striker to be repatriated. Tan said, "Cardiff City will continue to work with the AAIB and investigators to find out how the crash happened and to assist Emiliano's family. We have offered to them to arrange to take Emiliano back to rest with his family in Argentina. Even though he will be there his soul will always be in our hearts. We feel a tremendous loss but the biggest loss is borne by Sala's family."

An inquest at Bournemouth town hall had heard that the footballer died of head and trunk injuries just before his body was repatriated ahead of a wake at his boyhood club. Julio Muller, mayor of the town of Progreso in the Argentinian province of Santa Fe confirmed his remains would reach Ezeiza International Airport in Buenos Aires around 9am local time. The body would then be taken to the provincial capital by road on a six-hour journey before reaching Progreso for the wake at the San Martin Club gym.

Muller said Emiliano's mother Mercedes and sister Romina, who travelled to Europe, had already rejoined his father Horacio in Progreso. San Martin President Daniel Ribero added, "Emi's body is going to reach Argentina from Europe on Friday and on

Saturday we will spend several hours saying farewell to him at the club." San Martin de Progreso posted an emotional tribute on Facebook, saying, "We are waiting for you... like the first day you left but this time to stay with us forever. You went and you are an example for everyone. Eternally in our hearts." TV pictures showed a van carrying the body being slowly escorted out of Buenos Aires airport by police vehicles.

Neil Warnock, chief executive Ken Choo, and the club's Player Liaison Officer were among those attending the funeral. Choo was surprised to spot Willie McKay on the same flight out, a few rows in front of him. Warnock went over for a chat. Cardiff did not have a game that weekend as they were out of the FA Cup.

Ouest France reported that Nantes would be represented by central defender Nicolas Pallois and general secretary Loic Morin. Pallois, a close friend of Sala, missed Nantes' Ligue 1 game at Monaco to attend. Sala's family took the decision to cremate Emi's body so it was returning to the crematorium in the city of Santa Fe.

On the return journey to Wales, the Cardiff delegation were accosted at the airport by Willie McKay, who allegedly made death threats. The confrontation was partially witnessed by Neil Warnock, once again putting the manager in an invidious position. Managers need to keep agents onside but as he is an employee of Cardiff and McKay and his club were at loggerheads, even more so following the threats to their CEO Ken Choo as witnessed by the club's liaison officer. Witness statements were eventually taken and presented to South Wales police. Ken Choo was not taking the threats seriously and a source at the club said that there was "extra security" as it was supposed that Choo had body guards in attendance.

This and a series of alleged death threats to others connected with the investigation into the Sala transfer formed the basis of a series of exclusive revelations in the *Telegraph*.

6: THE AFTERMATH

THE *TELEGRAPH* LED THE WAY IN BREAKING the story that Cardiff City were contemplating a negligence case against Nantes. They felt that under French law, the fact that Willie McKay was operating on behalf of Nantes to facilitate the transfer together with his son Mark, and then to organise the fateful flight, that Nantes could be legally held liable for "negligence".

In a statement, Cardiff City told the *Telegraph*, "Cardiff has made its position very clear that it had nothing to do with the arrangements of the flight, and now new information is coming in every day as we are continuing to investigate the chain of events and the cause of the accident. We are looking at the potential possibility of negligence that may have caused the accident."

Cardiff City may sue Nantes for negligence if pilot in Emiliano Sala crash had incorrect licence

Ben Rumsby Tom Morgan, sports news correspondent Harry Harris

17 FEBRUARY 2019

Cardiff City could launch a negligence claim against Nantes as soon as this week if an official report finds Emiliano Sala was flown to his death by a pilot who did not have the correct licence. Senior figures at Cardiff are bracing themselves for an escalation in a legal row that saw them given until the end of last week to pay the first instalment of his £15 million transfer fee. Sala was buried on Saturday in his hometown of Progreso in Argentina, with Cardiff manager Neil Warnock among the mourners.

As first revealed by the *Telegraph*, Cardiff have frozen all payments while they wait for answers about how their record signing died and whether anyone could be held liable. Some of those answers could be provided this week, the Air Accidents Investigations Bureau having said it intended to publish an interim report into the January 21 crash within a month of it occurring.

Cardiff have also conducted an internal investigation that the *Telegraph* has been told has found no evidence pilot Dave Ibbotson held the licence necessary to carry passengers on a commercial basis. Senior figures believe, if the AAIB confirms Ibbotson was not qualified for the trip, that would constitute negligence on the part of whoever recruited the part-time gas engineer.

They also believe liability for that could be extended to cover Willie and Mark McKay who admitted arranging Sala's flight but not selecting the plane or pilot and, in turn, Nantes, for whom the duo had been working.

A successful negligence claim against the French club would slash the transfer fee owed to them for the player, the withholding of which they have threatened legal action over. Cardiff could attempt to reduce the figure further by arguing the change of ownership of Sala was incomplete when he died because he had yet to be registered to play in the Premier League. Chairman Mehmet Dalman told the *Telegraph*: "We believe that the player was not registered with the Premier League."

It can also be revealed that Cardiff broke their transfer record to sign Sala despite major concerns about the deal at boardroom level. More than one source has told this newspaper that City's four-man transfer committee was split over buying the striker, with a vote ending 3-1 in favour of doing so.

When asked by the *Telegraph* about the split, Dalman said: "I really don't think it is appropriate for me to comment at this stage but your line of enquiry is not necessarily wrong!"

EXCLUSIVE: *Emiliano Sala signed potentially invalid contract with Cardiff City*

Ben Rumsby Tom Morgan, sports news correspondent and Harry Harris

20 FEBRUARY 2019

Emiliano Sala signed a potentially invalid contract with Cardiff City in the days before he died in a plane crash, the *Daily Telegraph* can reveal.

Lawyers working on behalf of England's top tier have written to the Welsh club this week confirming their record signing was not fully registered to play in the competition last month.

The remarkable latest twist further muddies a legal row over whether Cardiff should pay Nantes the full £15million transfer. Sala's problematic contract came to light after Cardiff sought clarification as part of their attempt to stave off threatened legal action from Nantes over the freezing of payments.

The *Telegraph* understands Sala's Cardiff contract was deemed non-compliant with Premier League rules and was returned to them for him to sign an amended one. Neither the club nor the league would comment last night on the nature of the documentary discrepancies, although it is understood such issues are not uncommon.

Cardiff plan to use Sala's Premier League registration status to argue he was not their player when he died almost a month ago. They have also written to Nantes seeking evidence the French club had fully de-registered the Argentinian prior to the January 21 crash.

As of Wednesday, Nantes had yet to carry out threats issued

earlier this month of legal action against Cardiff if the latter did not pay the first instalment of Sala's transfer fee.

The Welsh club are continuing to build a negligence case against their French counterparts over the plane crash and are understood to want Sala's family to join them. More than one source said their case had been strengthened by an explosive interview given by Willie McKay to the *Telegraph* this week in which he confirmed his agent son, Mark, had been contracted to work for Nantes.

The McKays, who helped broker Sala's deal, arranged his trips to Cardiff and back during transfer talks and the club plan to hold Nantes vicariously liable as a result if an official report finds any flight regulations were breached on January 21. That could include rules governing safety equipment.

Relations between Cardiff and McKay Snr have deteriorated to such an extent that the club have written to him warning they reserve the right to deny him entry to their ground.

Cardiff have also snubbed a request by him for a public meeting about the Sala saga with owner Vincent Tan, chairman Mehmet Dalman, chief executive Ken Choo and manager Neil Warnock.

On Wednesday, both Nantes and the McKays found themselves at the centre of unrelated tax wrangles. Inspectors searched club premises at Nantes on Tuesday as an evasion investigation was launched by the National Public Prosecutor against the club's president, Waldemar Kita. Nantes were not immediately able to comment.

Meanwhile, a High Court hearing in London heard how Mercato Sports Ltd, a business registered in the names of Mark McKay and Willie McKay's wife, had cleared a tax debt in a last-gasp bid to fend off an HM Revenue and Customs winding up order.

The McKay family business was mentioned briefly at the Insolvency and Bankruptcy Court at the Rolls Building in central London. A barrister for HMRC told the court: "The debt has been paid. The petition is dismissed with costs."

Sala, whose body was recovered from plane wreckage two weeks ago, died from "head and trunk injuries". The pilot, David

Ibbotson, is still missing but searches are set to be resumed for his body.

EXCLUSIVE: *Cardiff City accuse Nantes of breaking FIFA rules over Emiliano Sala transfer*

Ben Rumsby Harry Harris

16 APRIL 2019

Cardiff City have accused Nantes of breaking FIFA rules over the tragic transfer of Emiliano Sala in their feud over his £15 million fee.

The *Daily Telegraph* can disclose details of the case Cardiff submitted to football's world governing body on Monday to explain their withholding of the first instalment of the fee for the striker, who was killed in a plane crash almost three months ago.

As previously revealed by the *Telegraph*, the Premier League club told FIFA the deal they struck to buy the striker became "null and void" after he died because he signed a contract deemed non-compliant with Premier League rules and legally-binding clauses in their transfer agreement with Nantes had not been fulfilled.

But a source with knowledge of Cardiff's submission confirmed yesterday it also accused Nantes of failing to disclose to FIFA's Transfer Matching System that the agent Mark McKay had been acting for them in the deal.

Annexe 3 of the governing body's Regulations on the Status and Transfer of Players (RSTP) states clubs must input the club intermediary's name and commission into its TMS.

The source told the *Telegraph*: The omission potentially impacts on the validity of the International Transfer Certificate and clearly constitutes a breach of Annexe 3 RSTP, rendering Nantes liable to sanction.

The same regulations require the uploading of "a copy of the contract between the new club and the professional player", something Cardiff were unable to do because Sala was killed before a revised one could be signed.

The source also revealed Cardiff's submission to FIFA laid out the circumstances around Sala's death and warned Nantes could be held vicariously liable for his plane crash.

The player's fatal flight was booked by McKay's father, Willie, who has also admitted helping his son conclude the transfer.

Article 1242 of the French Civil code states: "We are liable not only for the damage we cause by our own actions, but also for the damage caused by the actions of the people for whom we are responsible, or the things we have in our custody."

Nantes, who ignored a written invitation from Cardiff for a meeting to resolve their feud over Sala's transfer fee, declined to comment on whether they breached FIFA rules but indicated they would fight any attempt to hold them liable for his death.

McKay snr did not respond to requests for comment.

He has previously denied responsibility for Sala's death, stating he had no input into the selection of the fatal flight's pilot or aircraft.

7: THE PROFUSION OF AGENTS

JEROME ANDERSON, ONE OF THE BIGGEST NAMES of his generation of football agents, once told me that it was wrong to assume that he had pocketed £40m from a series of transfers he had orchestrated for Blackburn Rovers following the Lancashire club's takeover by the Indian-based VH Group in 2010. He explained that in one deal he had to facilitate payments to no less than nine agents who had an interest in the transfer. The reason is that there are quite a few agents who have contracts with either the player, the buying club or the selling club and others who help smooth through the activities of the main agents involved. With this in mind, the Emiliano Sala transfer is just one of many transfers where the flow of money and the individuals involved is far from transparent. So just who was involved in this transfer and how much did they stand to earn from the deal?

Mercato Sports Agency was set up in 2017, and this was the company named on the contract with Nantes signed by their president and counter signed by Mark McKay, who owned the agency. Meïssa N'Daiaye was Sala's agent, and he founded Sport Cover in 2006, and they also represent Cardiff's Sol Mamba, Manchester City full-back Benjamin Mendy and Chelsea centre forward Michy Batshuayi among others. McKay and N'Daiaye should have been the principal agents. Yet, Willie McKay was very much a major presence in the background despite being barred as an active middleman. However it became even more complicated with other names being bandied around as also being involved such as Bakari Sanogo, who is reported as being an influence on Nantes president Waldemar Kita and represents Tottenham's Moussa Sissoko. Then there is Baba Drame who works with the McKays and was involved in West Ham's £22m deal for Issa Diop from Toulouse. He posted his involvement with the Sala move to

Cardiff on Instagram. So that's five agents potentially involved in this one deal and presumably all of them are due a piece of Sala's transfer fee!

In the aftermath of the tragedy, Willie McKay denied claims of corruption and said he wanted a public meeting with press and Cardiff officials in order to clear his name. He told *The Sun*: "'We have nothing to hide, the rumours are f★★★★★★ c★★★, absolutely f★★★★★★ c★★★. I'm sick of it. I'm shocked people are saying this. I'm waiting for the FA to phone me. I want a public meeting with everybody there and you can chair it; Sky, the papers, everybody can come."

McKay had been the focus of media attention after organising several flights for Sala and Cardiff as the deal progressed, including the Piper Alpha plane that crashed, killing the player. He added, "The AAIB know the plane was not owned by me. Why won't the owner come forward? They have probably seen the abuse I am getting."

Football continues to attract colourful characters such as Nantes president Waldemar Kita who owns a penis enlargement company, although in fairness according to Wikipedia he made his fortune "manufacturing intra-ocular lenses for cataract surgery and in the treatment of glaucoma." In the middle of the row with Cardiff City over Sala, the offices of French side Nantes were raided by authorities in France, the premises in the club's home city and in Paris were targeted by national financial prosecutors. The Paris National Public Prosecutor's Office confirmed the opening of an investigation amid reports that their investigations centred on an alleged tax evasion case that police described as Kita's "personal tax situation".

Meanwhile Cardiff continued to seek more details of McKay's tie-up with Nantes and their owner. Warnock was sure his club would "take care" of the problem of the first instalment of the fee payable to Nantes. "I'm sure the club will take care of it in the coming days, because [chairman Mehmet Dalman] asked for an extension and Nantes has agreed. On reflection, I think certain things were done that should not have been done. That stirred everyone up. It created stories that shouldn't have been there." Warnock was referring to the situation of Sala's invalid Cardiff contract but the Cardiff manager wasn't above suspicion himself as we shall see...

As part of our investigations, Ben Rumsby was in constant touch with Willie McKay; either sending him notifications of pending articles or giving him the right of reply. These messages were usually ignored, but occasionally prompted an agitated call. On one such occasion McKay had something to get off his chest and was happy to talk to Ben on the record which turned out to be one of the key interviews in this sordid saga. Clearly the press scrutiny had got to him; Willie McKay was a man more suited to operating in the shadows. Someone accustomed to pulling the strings rather than showing his face in public. Now, with a bankruptcy case in the offing and his implication in the death of one of his clients making headline news he sought to set the record straight.

The Scot opened up to Ben Rumsby, accusing Cardiff City of "trying to throw me under the bus" as his bitter recriminations intensified. He lashed out at the owner, chairman and chief executive of the Welsh club claiming they were attempting to shift blame on to "an easy target". As Ben pointed out in his landmark interview reprinted below, McKay was retaliating to a *Telegraph* exclusive that the club were considering a negligence claim, and McKay knew that what was suggested put him in the frame if, as expected, an official report found the pilot did not have the correct licence.

To add extra fuel to McKay's over heated temperature, Cardiff were also prepared to sue the agent personally over his self-confessed bid to "create an interest" in the player and artificially raise the price. With FIFA and the police likely to be called in to investigate and with payments to Nantes frozen, which in turn meant payments to the McKays being frozen, Willie was not in the best of moods.

McKay did what he does best. He came out fighting insisting his "conscience was clear" and revealing he was "livid" over his treatment, accusing Cardiff owner Vincent Tan, chairman Mehmet Dalman and chief executive Ken Choo saying "Cardiff City have shown no class at all."

McKay provided *Telegraph* Sport with the contract between Nantes and his agent son, Mark, which confirmed the latter was due 10 per cent of any transfer fee - around £1.5m. The document also stipulates that McKay Jnr must "make every effort to ensure the French club receive the full amount of that fee as soon as possible".

McKay confirmed that he had spoken to the Air Accidents Investigations Branch (AAIB) about Sala's fatal journey, producing a timeline of all previous private-jet trips arranged as part of the transfer. This timeline, which he shared with *Telegraph* Sport, shows his son had organised and paid for two earlier flights to Nantes for Cardiff manager Neil Warnock to watch the striker and two between the cities for the player himself, the first for contract talks and the second for his medical.

McKay said: "The only flight everybody is talking about is the one that crashed, right? Cardiff knew everything [about every flight]. When are they going to come out and tell the truth?"

McKay confirmed that none of the four previous journeys used the same Piper Malibu plane or the pilot used on that fateful night. He claimed still not to know who owned the plane or whether David Ibbotson, who had £23,400 in County Court Judgments against him, was licensed to make a commercial flight or had been paid anything more than expenses. McKay said he routinely funded the flights and hotels of players he was contracted to sell and even managers he was trying to sell them to listing the practice among "gambles" he took in the hope of securing a lucrative pay-day.

He denied Sala had been overpriced, claiming Nantes were only due half his transfer fee because of a sell-on clause and that £15m actually "wasn't a good deal" for the French club.

Asked why he was even involved in that deal given he was declared bankrupt in 2015 and no longer held an intermediaries licence, McKay declared it was down to "nepotism" and to help "open some doors" for his son.

McKay attended Sala's funeral in Argentina, taking the same flight as Choo, and met the player's brother while there. "I met Emiliano the same amount of times as they [Cardiff officials] met him. I organised his flight. I tried to help him. They never tried to help him. They booked him one room at the St David's Hotel [in Cardiff]. That's all they've done for him. And they're trying to throw me under the bus."

Inside the world of Willie McKay -
the agent at the heart of the Emiliano Sala transfer

Willie McKay believes he is being made a scapegoat over a tragic sequence of events

Tom Morgan, sports news correspondent Ben Rumsby

24 FEBRUARY 2019

Jet-lagged, weary and sweltering under 30c clear blue skies, the burly Glaswegian in a heavy grey suit trudged towards the doorway of a makeshift chapel of rest in rural Argentina.

Willie McKay, his face shiny in the heat, had already driven 340 miles from Buenos Aires's Ministro Pistarini International Airport, six hours north along unfamiliar roads, eventually arriving at Emiliano Sala's remote hometown at 10am last Saturday.

The 36-hour round trip from London took him to a converted sports hall in Progreso, Santa Fe Province, where mourners were gathering to see Sala's coffin. Two security guards flanked the entrance as McKay walked in to the 1970s, bleached-white building to join the wake.

His solemn, respectful show was in stark contrast from the no-nonsense, bullish character who, just weeks earlier, had openly told Sala all he and his agent son cared about was "money". McKay, having launched foul-mouthed attacks against both Cardiff City officials and journalists in recent weeks, is now in need of allies.

As an unsavoury legal row simmers between Cardiff and Nantes over payment for the £15million Sala, McKay, 59, believes he is being made a scapegoat over a tragic sequence of events that led to the striker's death in the English Channel on Jan 21. To anyone who asks, McKay complains he has been "thrown under the bus" by Cardiff.

Nothing he did in the Sala deal is new and, for years, he has made no secret of his money-making operation. His *modus operandi* is simple: cream off the best talent in France and find a wealthy suitor in the Premier League. Or, as he wrote in his sales pitch to Sala on January 6: "We are not interested in looking after your personal interests, finance, holidays, baby-sitting… we do transfers."

However, Cardiff are now cutting ties and are even considering legal action against the man who has confirmed via leaked correspondence how he muscled in on the deal, created a "buzz" and now, thank you very much, says his son Mark is due a 10 per cent cut.

McKay has, for years, no longer been subject to the Football Association regulation. Having been made bankrupt in 2015, his son, Mark, 32, and his wife, Janis, 58, now officially run the family business. His explanation for his ongoing involvement in affairs is "nepotism". Despite handing over the keys to the business to Mark, McKay Snr is still living handsomely.

His last-known address is a sprawling mansion which was bought by Mark in 2017 for £1.4million. McKay no longer owns racehorses, but the 35 acre grounds off the six-bedroom farmhouse are an enthusiast's dream, with an all-weather track with a half-mile gallop, 27 stables, tack and feed rooms.

McKay says he has been involved in 600 deals, largely thanks to his strong links with high-profile managers, mostly generated during the early years of the Premier League. Among those at the end of the phone have been Neil Warnock and Harry Redknapp. Cardiff boss Warnock, who denies being "big pals" with McKay, recently told *Telegraph* Sport: "If you want to get the job done, then you need the Willie McKays of this world." But he also added: "Someone suggested that if I went to Sala's funeral that Willie McKay would be standing alongside me. That was just distasteful."

Indeed, while Warnock and officials from Cardiff were conspicuous at last weekend's wake in the small town of Progreso, Santa Fe Province, McKay kept a low profile. He instead arrived with a friend to pay his own respects to Sala and also meeting the player's brother, Dario, who has led a humble existence, still living in the same town where he once kicked a ball about with a young Emiliano.

It was not the first time in his career the Scot had found himself unwanted baggage. Over the years, he has had scrapes with police, footballing authorities and the tax man, but always insisted - often with an expletive or two - that he was a wronged man.

Back in 2008, McKay was handed a suspended ban by the FA after being found guilty of breaking transfer rules during Benjani Mwaruwari's moves from French club Auxerre to Portsmouth and from Portsmouth to Manchester City. The ill-fated City switch went down in transfer-deadline-day folklore after it was claimed the striker fell asleep at Southampton Airport and missed two flights north to Manchester. In the ensuing fallout, Portsmouth were fined £15,000, Benjani was cleared by the FA and McKay was found guilty of flouting regulations which did not allow agents to act for two different clubs, in two consecutive transactions, involving the same player.

McKay's reaction to it all was a familiar theme. "I think it's a witch-hunt and I'm not going to deviate from that," he said.

He had been equally incandescent after being arrested in November 2007, but never charged, by City of London Police's

Economic Crime Department on suspicion of conspiracy to defraud and false accounting. A long-running investigation linked to Redknapp - then manager of Portsmouth - and Milan Mandaric would eventually end up in court. Five years later, a jury would throw out the case brought over two deposits, totalling US$295,000 (£183,000), paid into a Monaco bank account. Afterwards, McKay told *Telegraph* Sport of a conspiracy against his profession. "It's easy to go after football agents," he said. "Nobody likes football agents."

His roller-coaster business ventures continued unabated. He played a key role in getting Joey Barton a restorative loan move to Marseille after the midfielder was handed a 12-match ban while at QPR for attacking several Manchester City players on the final day of the 2011-12 Premier League campaign.

That same season also saw an ill-fated experiment at hometown club Doncaster Rovers. McKay helped entice a number of high-profile players to the Keepmoat Stadium. They included El-Hadji Diouf, Pascal Chimbonda, Habib Beye and Freddie Piquionne, signed on reduced wages thanks to McKay's international contacts. The project was abandoned after Doncaster were relegated from the Championship, ironically following defeat to Portsmouth.

That August, things turned from bad to worse when McKay was stopped while using his mobile phone as he drove down Pall Mall in central London. Officers discovered he was banned from driving at the time and found cocaine in the car. He was branded "arrogant" by a judge, fined £6,000 for driving illegally and cautioned over the Class A drug.

Then, in April 2015, he was declared bankrupt at a hearing in Glasgow. At the time, McKay revealed assets of just £987, while court documents detailed that he owed £713,292.

He was discharged from bankruptcy last August, agreeing to a five-year restriction order prohibiting him from being a director or managing a company, without permission from a court.

McKay, it would seem, has always thought the football world was out to get him, but questions surrounding his involvement in the flight that tragically took Sala's life have left him simmering with rage. "We just tried to help the boy," he says.

His involvement in bringing the 28-year-old to the Premier League traces back much longer than Cardiff's official interest in the player. McKay was optimistic about getting the Argentinian a big-money deal and says he even got on the phone to Liverpool's chief scout. "I said to Barry Hunter, 'Why don't you take him? He's a great player for you coming off the bench'." He also insists West Ham United were interested in Sala "but they weren't interested at 25 million Euros."

Cardiff are understood to be enraged that McKay could have pushed up the player's price by planting stories, but he denies his meddling made Sala more expensive. There is also lingering anger between the club and McKay over the arrangements for Sala's doomed trip on the single-engined Piper Malibu plane, piloted by a part-time gas engineer, but the Scot vehemently insists his "conscience is clear". He explains there were multiple flights backwards and forwards from Cardiff to Nantes in the weeks before the tragedy " none which was questioned". On December 5, he made arrangements for Warnock, the manager's assistant Kevin Blackwell, and him and his son, Mark, to watch Nantes play Marseille. He then arranged Sala's flight from France to Cardiff on January 18 for his medical at his new club.

However, over that same weekend, when Sala was due to say his goodbyes to his team-mates in France, McKay's usual pilot, David Henderson, and another called David Hayman who had initially flown Sala over to Wales appear to have been busy. "The guy who brought Sala over on the Friday morning couldn't take him back because he was at a 40th birthday party in Bakewell," said McKay.

A long-awaited interim report by the Air Accidents Investigations Branch is likely to clear up lingering questions about the crash when it is published on Monday. McKay is convinced he will finally be absolved of any blame and insists he had no say in Dave Ibbotson, whose body is still missing, ending up at the doomed plane's controls.

Given his status as a bankrupt and unofficial deal-maker, McKay's conduct is likely to focus minds at FIFA, which was already looking at introducing tougher rules on intermediaries. Greg Clarke, the FA chairman, refused to comment on the Sala case, but has confirmed he would work closely with the world governing body after being elected one of its vice-presidents.

"I'm an easy target," says McKay. After decades of toothless attempts by footballing authorities better to scrutinise agents, that target may now be coming into their cross hairs.

Following the *Telegraph* interview, Willie McKay went on something of a charm offensive sitting down with BBC News Sports Editor Dan Roan later that week to make his case before a wider audience. Once more he insisted that his "conscience is clear" adding that he had organised multiple flights backwards and forwards from Cardiff to Nantes in the weeks before the tragedy, "none of which was questioned."

"I wish to make clear that despite media reports today, the plane involved in this terrible episode was not owned in any way or part by either myself or any member of my family. I can confirm that when Emiliano made myself and his agent Meïssa N'Diaye aware that he wished to travel back to Nantes following his medical and signing on Friday, I began to look into arranging a private flight to take him to Nantes on Saturday morning. That evening, it was confirmed a plane was available to fly Emiliano on Saturday which could remain in Nantes until he was due to return to Cardiff.

"I have been in contact with officials from Cardiff City FC and the player's agent over these difficult past few days and will continue to do so. I have chosen to wait a few days before making a statement so that the focus remained on the efforts of the search and rescue teams looking for Emiliano Sala and the pilot of the missing plane. Along with everyone in the world of football, I want to express my sadness and that of my family with regards to the tragic events that have unfolded since Monday evening.

"The families of both Emiliano and that of the pilot are

utmost in our thoughts and prayers. I knew Emiliano well, he was a wonderful person and I count myself fortunate to have known him."

Describing the time period since the crash, McKay told *L'Equipe* that it has "been an absolute nightmare for us." He said that if he had not allowed Sala to return to his old club, Nantes, to say goodbye to his former teammates and put his beloved dog in kennels "'he would still be with us".

Meanwhile the pilot originally named on the flight plan, David Henderson, had gone into hiding and his daughter complained to the Press Commission to seek a preventative order for the media to cease harassing him, as he was inundated, naturally, for interviews when it emerged that his name had been on the original flight plan of the plane returning from Nantes to Cardiff, and he was the one at first announced missing presumed dead by French media. Clearly the authorities were keen for a full explanation of why he passed the flight on to another pilot, and how much of that detail was known to Willie McKay.

McKay also said that he had met with Sala's friends and family to "give them an understanding of how Emiliano came to be on that plane", adding, "the tragic events that have unfolded have shocked us all".

The *Telegraph* broke the story that Cardiff City launched an internal investigation into the circumstances ahead of a potential negligence claim against McKay; they clearly felt that, as the Scot was due a 10% fee from the transfer, he was acting on behalf of Nantes and liability had yet to be determined. McKay was furious with Cardiff's stance.

The club faced enormous losses, possibly as much as £14m - even with insurance payouts although even that was now in doubt. The club's accident policy was led by China Re Syndicate 2088, with Sala's name likely to have been added to the club's policy when his transfer was completed. The player's contract, which was originally thought to have been signed and sealed two days before Sala's disappearance, had in fact been returned by the Premier League and the club made it clear he wasn't their player. A source at the club told me "they can hardly have a player insured who technically was not their player as his contract had been declared null and void by the Premier League!"

Players are automatically enrolled onto the Professional Footballers' pension scheme when they sign a contract in England. This is then registered with the appropriate football authorities and makes provision for a £600,000 maximum compensation fee to relatives for 'death-in-service'. The Professional Footballers' pension scheme is not a PFA scheme but the PFA are trustees, along with the Premier League, EFL and independent trustees. The PFA planned to call on the pension fund to honour the payment as Sala had already signed his contract with Cardiff, even though that contract was now the centre of a dispute with Cardiff claiming it was 'null and void'.

John Bramhall, the PFA deputy chief executive, told *The Times*, "It will be for the trustees to see whether they are able to make the payment from there. Normally it would be a simple process but we will be speaking with them on this. Usually, as soon as a contract is registered with the Premier League the player is enrolled on the pension scheme." The family of former Newcastle United midfielder Cheick Tioté received £600,000 from the fund after he died while training at Beijing Enterprises in June 2017, his place in the pension fund was still valid despite playing in China as his death came within six months of leaving St James' Park.

Yet the status of the contract was now central to Cardiff's case against Nantes, which would have put the £600,000 payment in jeopardy. However much the PFA might recommend the money is paid out, it is a decision for the trustees and with so many legal complications, it is likely to be on hold until those issues are resolved.

The Welsh club were 'increasingly concerned' about a number of issues, besides the financial implications, and payments to Nantes were therefore frozen, Cardiff insisting that they "will pay whatever is due only when they had established all the answers and can determine all the facts".

When Sala boarded that fatal flight his contractual situation was yet to be concluded. He was no doubt in a concerned state of mind, possibly others may also have been concerned with so much riding on the completion of the contractual detail before his signing satisfied Premier League rules. At the very least he would have had to sign a new contract, which would then have to be resubmitted to the Premier League for their approval before he could play in their competition, irrespective of the international clearance going through FIFA and the FA of Wales.

Cardiff had agreed a 20m euro transfer fee with Nantes to include 3m euros if the club survived relegation, over a three year period. As the *Daily Telegraph* investigation made clear, the Welsh club felt that when he stepped on that fatal flight he wasn't a Cardiff player. Yet Nantes were adamant that international clearance had gone through, and that he was no longer their player and that he belonged to Cardiff. Battle lines were drawn and FIFA would ultimately make a judgement.

The transfer fee was set to be paid in three instalments with Sala's agent Meïssa N'Diaye, due 7 per cent of the fees paid by Cardiff, and Mark McKay's company due 10 per cent of the fees including the bonuses for staying up, amounting to more than £2m. The final £30 million bill included Sala's £2million plus a year salary over three and a bit years. Cardiff also expected to lose money that could have come from shirt sales and sponsorship.

Between the undersigned:

FC NANTES SASP (professional sports limited company) with share capital of €500,000, registered in the Nantes Trade and Companies Register under no. 388 113 278, registered office Centre Sportif La Jonelière, 44240 La Chapelle sur Erdre, represented by Mr Franck KITA, duly authorised, in his capacity as Managing Director, hereinafter referred to as the "Club",

And:

Mr Mark MCKAY, managing director of MERCATO SPORTS LTD, registered under no. 10683175, registered office Martin Grange Lodge, Martin Common, Doncaster, DN10 6DD, sports agent authorised by the FFF to operate in French territory, hereinafter referred to as the "Agent",

Hereinafter jointly referred to as the "Parties"

WHEREAS

This contract is concluded in accordance and in compliance with Articles L222-5 to L222-22 and R222-1 to R222-42 of the French Code of Sport (*Code du sport*).

Mr Emiliano Sala, born 31/10/1900, of Italian and Argentine nationality (the "Player"), is bound by a fixed-term contract with the Club until 30 June 2022.

Several English clubs in the Premier League football championship have expressed their desire to obtain the Player's definitive transfer for the 2018/2019 season.

The Agent has developed knowledge, expertise and know-how in negotiating football player transfer agreements.

The Agent is therefore engaged to negotiate the final transfer of the Player to a football club in the Premier League football championship.

THE FOLLOWING HAS BEEN AGREED

CLAUSE 1: PURPOSE

The purpose of this agreement is to lay down the terms and conditions under which the Agent shall perform a negotiation and assistance engagement on behalf of the Club under the terms and conditions set out below.

FC NANTES

Registered office: Centre Sportif LA JONELLIERE – 44 240 LA CHAPELLE SUR ERDRE – Postal address: BP 51124 44 311 NANTES CEDEX 3
Tel: 02 40 37 29 00 – Fax: +33 (0)2 40 37 29 21 – E-mail: contact@fcnantes.com
SAS [sports limited company] to share capital of €500,000 – 388 113 278 NANTES TRADES & COMPANIES REGISTER – VAT FR 49 388 1 13 278

Under the terms of the contract between Nantes and Mark McKay, the agent will receive a 10 per cent of the transfer fee, but it will be dependent on the player has to be registered to be able to play in the Premier League before the commissions can be activated.

---

applicable in the event of a subsequent transfer of the Player and/or on the basis of any other contingent additional compensation that might be provided for in the definitive transfer agreement concluded between the Club and the club to which the Player is transferred under this Agreement or on the amount of any applicable Solidarity Contribution pursuant to the FIFA Regulations on the Status and Transfer of Players.

Clause 3.2: Payment terms

The amount of the services incumbent on the Agent under this agreement shall be the subject, at the Parties' convenience, of one or more invoices issued as from the approval by the Ligue de Football Professionnel of the contractual amendment terminating the Player's employment contract with the Club.

Payments shall be made by cheque or bank transfer at 30 days and of month from receipt of the invoice.

As part of his engagement, it is incumbent on the Agent to ensure that the definitive transfer fee negotiated is actually paid to the Club. Thus, in the event of the late payment or non-payment by the acquiring club of some or all of the definitive transfer fee, the Club reserves the right to pay the Agent his commission progressively as the Club actually collects some or all of the definitive transfer fee, without such conduct constituting a default that would render the Club liable towards to the Agent. The Agent shall make every effort to ensure that the Club is able to obtain payment of the full transfer fee as rapidly as possible.

The Agent alone shall be liable for his tax and social security obligations in relation to the aforesaid payment and under no circumstances shall claims for liability or claims for payment be made against the Club in the event of the Agent's non-performance of his obligations towards any social security or tax bodies.

CLAUSE 4: AGENT'S REPRESENTATIONS AND UNDERTAKINGS – RESCISSION OF THE AGREEMENT

The Agent understands and assures the Club that he shall comply with the terms of French law and regulations pertaining to sports intermediaries, in particular the provisions of articles L.222-5 to L.222-22 and R222-1 to R222-42 of the French Code of Sport, and with the regulations laid down by the Fédération Internationale du Football Association (FIFA) and the Fédération Française de Football (FFF). The Agent also represents and expressly acknowledges that he is not aware of any event that might jeopardise the licence authorising him to exercise the profession of sports agent pursuant to Articles L.222-5 to L.222-22 and R222-1 to R222-42 of the French Code of Sport and to fulfil the obligations incumbent upon him under this Agreement.

Compliance with the representations and undertakings provided for in this clause of this Agreement constitutes an essential and determining condition of the undertakings given by the Club, in particular its financial undertakings towards the Agent, and any breach thereof shall justify the immediate rescission as of right of this Agreement.

Such rescission shall entail the restoration of the Parties to the situation prior to the signing of this agreement, and shall therefore entail repayment by the Agent of any payments already made to him by the Club on the date on which said rescission takes place.

CLAUSE 5: TERM

This contract takes effect as from its signing and shall end on 2 February 2019 if on that date no definitive transfer agreement for the Player has been concluded with a club in the Premier League football

FC NANTES

Registered office: Centre Sportif LA JONELLIERE – 44 240 LA CHAPELLE SUR ERDRE – Postal address: BP 51124 44 311 NANTES CEDEX 3
Tel: 02 40 37 29 00 – Fax: +33 (0)2 40 37 29 21 – E-mail: contact@fcnantes.com
SAS [sports limited company] to share capital of €500,000 – 388 113 278 NANTES TRADES & COMPANIES REGISTER – VAT FR 49 388 1 13 278

8: THE PILOT

AVID IBBOTSON WAS A 60-YEAR-OLD FATHER-of-four, a devoted family man, loved by his family and by all accounts a decent enough chap from Scunthorpe. At the time this book went to press, he was still missing presumed dead. The question hanging over him in the aftermath of the crash surrounded his qualifications to take a commercial flight. It had emerged that he was in debt and presumably under pressure to take the flight for financial reasons, even if it that meant cutting corners. Flights are deemed commercial if the cost of the flight is paid for by the passengers rather being shared with the pilot.

It later emerged that Ibbotson was colour blind and barred from flying at night so should not have been piloting a single-engined plane over the Channel at night during winter. A part-time DJ and gas engineer, the Scunthorpe man was also an occasional pilot who touted for odd flying jobs on Facebook and had four outstanding county court judgments against him totalling £18,000 at the time of the crash. He had 3,500 hours of flying experience, of which 30 were flying similar types of aircraft to the one in which he made the fatal journey but when he pitched up to take the plane from Cardiff to Nantes he confessed that he was "rusty" with the controls of the 35-year-old plane having flown just 20 hours in the 90 days before the crash, and seven hours in the previous 28 days.

The Sun revealed that he once crashed a plane on the runway after failing to lower its landing gear, writing off a Piper Cherokee with a belly flop on an exercise simulating an engine failure in 1995. An AAIB report did not name him but sources confirmed it was Ibbotson, according to *The Sun*. He held a basic private pilot's licence and 246 hours of flying experience when he took the Cherokee up at Hibaldstow Airfield on May 9 1995. The Department for Transport, which runs the AAIB, refused to comment on individuals and Skydive Hibaldstow did not respond to calls.

Originally David Henderson was supposed to have been piloting the ill-fated plane. His name was on a flight plan submitted to Nantes airport on the day of the journey before it was cancelled and replaced with a second plan with Ibbotson named as the pilot. Following the crash, French media reported Henderson as missing following the disappearance of the Piper Malibu PA-46 near the Channel Islands - a reasonable mistake considering that he was registered as the pilot for the flight.

Henderson later took to Facebook to confirm he was alive. He often flew skydivers to jump sites, and belonged to three 'ferry flight' Facebook groups where companies advertise flying jobs. He had previously worked for Mark McKay - son of agent Willie McKay - who played a part in arranging Sala's flight, before using the same plane. He had flown Nice FC general manager Julien Fournier from Surrey to the French port of Marseille in the single-engined US-registered Piper a year earlier.

Henderson drafted in Ibbotson to replace him to take Sala to Nantes because he was unavailable asking him, "Do you want to spend a weekend in Nantes?" Ibbotson stayed in the £68-a-night Hotel Kyriad for two nights before the flight. He booked a taxi to take him from his hotel to the airport at 7.30am on Monday January 21 so that he could make the return journey but cancelled the morning taxi and checked back into his hotel room where he stayed for the day. He then left the hotel for Nantes Bouaye Aeroport at 6pm for the evening flight. "Mr Ibbotson asked me to book him a taxi to take him to the airport at 7.30 am on Monday morning," a receptionist at the hotel told the *Daily Mail*. "He told me the flight from Nantes to Cardiff was scheduled to leave on Monday morning".

The return flight was delayed for ten hours before starting its doomed journey, and eventually took off late in the evening. With Ibbotson barred from night flying as he was colour blind, he knew he shouldn't fly and Aviation authorities later confirmed that Ibbotson did not have a 'night rating' on his UK private pilot permit. A source said, "Flying outside the restrictions of your licence is illegal and that's likely to affect the insurance cover for the flight." Ibbotson may have breached the terms of his licence as European regulations define night-time as "the time from half an hour after sunset until half an hour before sunrise."

David Henderson's passport had been scanned by security at Nantes Airport on the day of the flight to Cardiff, according to reports in the French media at the time. However at the time he categorically denied any involvement with Sala's flight claiming, "I have not been to Nantes for one year." Asked why his passport was scanned by security at Nantes Airport on Monday January 21 at the same time as Sala and replacement pilot Ibbotson passed through security Henderson told the newspaper, "I cannot explain their [French airport security's] mistake."

Henderson had been the subject of a BBC Radio 4 documentary in 2015 which told the stories of 'ferry pilots' who fly single-engined planes across the Atlantic going via Wick in Scotland, Iceland, Greenland and down through Canada. Interestingly, these planes were modified to include a life raft in the event that they were forced to ditch in the ocean because single-engined craft were not designed to fly over large bodies of water. It is unknown whether the plane carrying Emiliano Sala contained a life raft.

When the AAIB released chilling images of the stricken plane under the sea two weeks after it vanished, police officers visited Ibbotson's wife Nora to inform her that a body had been found at the bottom of the English Channel, although it was later identified as that of Sala.

A few days later Nora and her daughter spoke to breakfast TV show Good Morning Britain. The pair said they would never give up hope of finding him, as an inquest was opened and adjourned. A fundraising campaign to restart the search for Ibbotson raised more than £150,000 of a £300,000 target. Speaking on the show his daughter Danielle said her father would not give up looking for her if she was missing, so she would not give up on him "If you've got hope then you shouldn't give up," she said, "he wouldn't stop searching for me. We still hope and pray and hope everyone keeps my dad in their prayers." Good Morning Britain viewers later criticised Richard Madeley after a controversial interview, after he asked why they want to find his dead body.

A Go Fund Me page was set up which read, "Please help bring David Ibbotson home and help give him the send off he deserves. As a family we are relying on the kindness of the good-hearted people to help us raise the much needed funds to help us find our beloved Dad, Husband and Son. As a family we are trying to come to terms with the tragedy and the loss of two incredible men. To be told the search has now been called off for the foreseeable future has only made this tragic time more difficult. We can not bare the thought of him being alone, we need him home so that we are able to lay him to rest."

A donation from Gary Lineker of £1,000 is registered on the page, which he shared with his 7.2 million Twitter followers. A £27,000 donation under the name Elie Lottin, apparently made by France's World Cup winning footballer Kylian Sanmi Mbappé Lottin, is also listed. Vincent Tan donated £50,000 to the fund to resume search efforts for missing pilot. Tan had already offered to help Sala's family fly his body home to Argentina. He said, "Cardiff City will continue to work with the Air Accident Investigation Branch and investigators to find out how the crash happened and to assist Emiliano's family. We have offered to them to arrange to take Emiliano back to rest with his family in Argentina. Even though he will be there his soul will always be in our hearts. We feel a tremendous loss but the biggest loss is borne by Sala's family. May Sala's soul rest in peace."

AAIB INTERIM REPORT IN FULL
FOUR KEY AREAS OF INVESTIGATION

Pilot Not Legally Licensed - Official Report

A preliminary report raised questions about whether the pilot, David Ibbotson, was legally licensed, with suspicions that he was not. An investigation into the crash focused on the validity of the pilot's licence. The AAIB named 'regulatory requirements' as one of four areas in which further work would be carried out.

Ibbotson was not licensed to fly commercially, and as Willie McKay had confessed to hiring the plane and paying all the costs, the likelihood is that it would be proven that the flight was illegal. Cardiff City felt this was one of the cornerstones of their case for withholding payment to Nantes as they considered the French club partially liable, as McKay was working on their behalf. A case of negligence was being worked on by Cardiff City lawyers.

The Air Accident Investigation Branch (AAIB) report confirmed that the Piper Malibu aircraft was not licensed for commercial use as Ibbotson was entitled to transport the player only on a private basis. But to do so he would have needed to pay at least half the operating costs of the flight, under aviation rules governing the carrying of passengers. The rules which allow non-commercial pilots to gain experience by take passengers on a 'cost sharing' basis, also dictate that he needed to have had 'a bona fide purpose for making the flight' other than carrying Sala. "The flight must not be made for the purpose of merely transporting the passenger," the AAIB report stated.

McKay, mandated by Nantes to find a buyer for Sala, had asked his regular first-choice pilot David Henderson to make the flight but he was unavailable. The AAIB, whose full report had yet to be published, would continue to investigate whether Ibbotson did comply with 'cost share' rules laid out by the US Federal Aviation Authority, with whom the craft was registered.

The interim report did not state who owns the aircraft, although a Derbyshire-based firm called Cool Flourish was at the centre of that aspect of the inquiry. The AAIB revealed that the plane had been subject to scheduled maintenance just a few months before with no problems, and was fitted with an ice protection system that allowed it to fly "into known icing conditions".

The report charts the course of the flight before the aircraft crashed, detailing how the Piper Malibu had climbed to 5,500ft. About 13 nautical miles south of Guernsey, Ibbotson asked for permission to descend to maintain "visual meteorological conditions". After doing so, air traffic control asked Ibbotson if he wished to descend further. He responded saying, "Negative, just avoided a patch there, but back on heading five thousand feet." Ten minutes later he made another request to descend. There were further descents and ascents, with the penultimate radar sighting suggested the plane may have dropped to 1,600ft.

The AAIB report stated: "It is thought that the pilot's license and logbook were lost with the aircraft and so the ratings on his licenses and their validity, and the extent of his recent flying have not yet been determined."

The aircraft remained underwater off the coast of Guernsey as the AAIB report revealed the aircraft shattered into three pieces, with previously unseen pictures published showing the wreckage of the plane. Investigators had yet to determine what caused the crash, but the plane was believed to have fallen thousands of feet in just 20 seconds after making a 180-degree turn. The wreckage was found 30 metres from its final recorded location on radar "at an altitude of 1,600ft", "leading to the conclusion it fell almost vertically".

The identity of the Piper Malibu's owner remained undisclosed, with the unnamed individual not applying for "permission to operate the aircraft commercially". The AAIB said ownership had been transferred into an American trust allowing it to be registered in the US. This trust had a contract with a UK company that originally bought the plane. The company was responsible for the operation of the aircraft, ensuring it was maintained in accordance

Farnborough House
Berkshire Copse Road
Aldershot, Hants GU11 2HH

Tel:01252 510300
Fax: 01252 376999
www.aaib.gov.uk

AAIB Bulletin S1/2019
SPECIAL

ACCIDENT

Aircraft Type and Registration:	Piper PA-46-310P Malibu, N264DB
No & Type of Engines:	1 Teledyne Continental TSIO-520-BE engine
Year of Manufacture:	1984 (Serial no: 46-8408037)
Date & Time (UTC):	21 January 2019 at 2016 hrs
Location:	22 nm north-north-west of Guernsey
Type of Flight:	Unknown
Persons on Board:	Crew - 1 Passengers - 1
Injuries:	Crew - 1 (Missing) Passengers - 1 (Fatal)
Nature of Damage:	Aircraft destroyed
Commander's Licence:	Private Pilot's Licence
Commander's Age:	59 years
Commander's Flying Experience:	Approximately 3,700 hours Last 90 days - unknown Last 28 days - unknown
Information Source:	AAIB Field Investigation

Introduction

At 2122 hrs on 21 January 2019, the AAIB was informed that a Piper PA-46-310P Malibu aircraft, registration N264DB, had been lost from radar in transit from Nantes, France, to Cardiff in the UK, and that a surface search for survivors was underway using assets from the Channel Islands, UK and France. The wreckage of the aircraft had not been located by the time the official search ended at 1515 hrs on 24 January 2019, and the event therefore became classed as an aircraft accident under the terms of Annex 13 to the Convention on International Civil Aviation[1]. There were two persons on board the aircraft but neither was found by the surface search.

Footnote

[1]   Annex 13 contains International Standards and Recommended Practices for Aircraft Accident and Incident Investigation.

The aircraft was lost in international waters and, in such circumstances, Annex 13 places a responsibility on the State of Registration of the aircraft, in this case the USA as represented by the National Transportation Safety Board (NTSB), to commence an investigation. However, the State of Registration may, by mutual agreement, delegate the investigation to another State. On 22 January 2019, in anticipation that an accident investigation would be required, the NTSB delegated responsibility for the investigation to the State of the Operator, in this case the UK as represented by the AAIB.

The AAIB began an investigation assisted by the Bureau d'Enquêtes et d'Analyses pour la Sécurité de l'Aviation Civile (BEA) in France, which had been supporting search activities since the accident occurred, the NTSB in the USA, and the Junta de Investigación de Accidentes de Aviación Civil (JIAAC) in Argentina.

This Special Bulletin contains preliminary factual information on the investigation and general information about how aircraft registered in the USA may be operated between the UK and France.

History of the flight

The pilot of N264DB flew the aircraft and a passenger from Cardiff Airport to Nantes Airport on 19 January 2019 with a return flight scheduled for 21 January 2019. The pilot arrived at the airport in Nantes at 1246 hrs on 21 January to refuel and prepare the aircraft for the flight. At 1836 hrs the passenger arrived at airport security, and the aircraft taxied out for departure at 1906 hrs. Figure 1 shows the aircraft on the ground before departure.

Figure 1

N264DB on the ground at Nantes prior to the flight

The pilot's planned route would take the aircraft on an almost direct track from Nantes to Cardiff, flying overhead Guernsey en route (Figure 2). The Visual Flight Rules (VFR) flight plan indicated a cruise altitude of 6,000 ft amsl[2] and a distance of 265 nm.

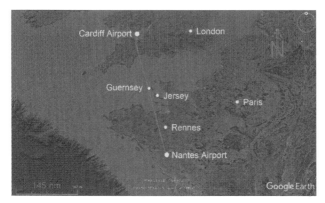

Figure 2

Planned route from Nantes to Cardiff

The aircraft took off from Runway 03 at Nantes Airport at 1915 hrs, and the pilot asked ATC for clearance to climb to 5,500 ft. The climb was approved by Nantes Approach Control and the flight plan was activated.

The aircraft flew on its planned route towards Cardiff until it was approximately 13 nm south of Guernsey when the pilot requested and was given a descent to remain in Visual Meteorological Conditions (VMC)[3]. Figure 3 shows the aircraft's subsequent track. The last radio contact with the aircraft was with Jersey Radar at 2012 hrs, when the pilot asked for a further descent. The aircraft's last recorded secondary radar point was at 2016:34 hrs, although two further primary returns were recorded after this[4]. The wreckage of N264DB was subsequently found on the seabed about 30 metres from the position of the last secondary radar point recorded by the radar at Guernsey.

Footnote

2   amsl: above mean sea level.

3   Pilots must remain in VMC to continue flight under Visual Flight Rules, the rules under which this flight was undertaken. The aircraft was in Class D airspace and so the pilot was required to remain 1,500 m horizontally and 1,000 ft vertically clear of cloud, and have an in-flight visibility greater than 5,000 m.

4   See later section, *Recorded information*, for an explanation of the radar data.

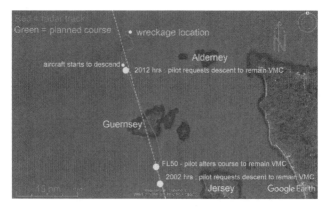

Figure 3

Aircraft track in the vicinity of Guernsey

Weather conditions

A weather forecast was issued by the Jersey Meteorological Department at 1502 hrs on 21 January 2019, valid for the period between 1600 hrs and 2200 hrs. This forecast showed a cold front moving in from the northwest, which was forecast to bring rain spreading in from the northwest overnight. The forecast included the possibility of isolated showers for the whole period of validity. Actual observations at Guernsey Airport for 1950 hrs showed that the visibility was in excess of 10 km and the cloud was FEW[5] at 1,000 ft above the level of the airfield (aal). At 2020 hrs, Guernsey was reporting light showers of rain and FEW clouds at 1,000 ft aal.

The rainfall radar picture at 2015 hrs showed a band of showers, some heavy, passing through the area of flight as shown in Figure 4.

Data from the UK Met Office indicated that the freezing level around the Channel Islands was between 3,000 ft and 4,000 ft amsl.

Footnote

[5] Cloud cover is often given in eighths of the sky covered, or oktas. FEW refers to 1-2 oktas of cloud which is 1-2 eighths of the sky covered.

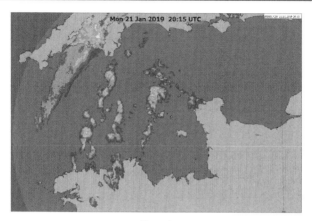

Figure 4
Rainfall radar for 2015 hrs

Aircraft description

The PA-46-310P Malibu is a single engine, all metal, low wing, pressurised aircraft fitted with retractable landing gear and a single turbocharged piston engine, driving a two-blade constant speed propeller. The primary flight controls are conventional in operation and are operated by cables. The aircraft is also equipped with four-position, hydraulically operated flaps, a stall warning device and an electrically heated pitot probe. The aircraft has a fuel capacity of 122 gal (US) stored in an integral fuel tank located in each wing.

N264DB was equipped with an ice protection system that allowed it to fly into known icing conditions. It was also fitted with avionic equipment that allowed it to be flown safely at night in Instrument Meteorological Conditions (IMC[6]).

The aircraft was equipped with six seats. The two forward passenger seats faced aft, and all passenger seats had adjustable backs with built-in headrests. The rearward facing passenger seats were equipped with lap straps and all the other seats with three-point harnesses (car style). Entry to the aircraft was through a rear door on the left side of the cabin. An emergency exit was located on the right side of the cabin behind the front seat. The aircraft was equipped with an Emergency Locator Transmitter (ELT) with a three-position switch: ON, OFF, ARMED. When selected to ARMED the ELT would automatically

Footnote

[6]   If meteorological conditions are less than the VMC limits detailed in Footnote 3, they are Instrument Meteorological Conditions and the aircraft must be operated in accordance with Instrument Flight Rules.

start to transmit when it detected an impact. ELT transmissions cannot be detected underwater. The aircraft was also equipped with life jackets for each occupant and a six-man life raft, kept in the rear baggage compartment and accessible from the cabin.

Aircraft history and maintenance

N264DB was manufactured in 1984, and on 30 November 2018 the airframe had flown 6,636 hrs and the engine had operated for 1,195 hrs since overhaul. The Certificate of Registration was issued on 11 September 2015 and had an expiry date of 30 September 2021. The Airworthiness Certificate was dated 27 April 1984. This certificate remains valid if aircraft maintenance has been performed in accordance with Federal Aviation Regulations (FAR) Parts 21, 43 and 91. The last significant maintenance was an Annual / 100-hour maintenance that was completed on 30 November 2018; the Certificate of Release to Service was signed by the holder of a Federal Aviation Administration (FAA) Inspector Authorization (IA).

Underwater search

Background

Following an aircraft accident at sea, an underwater search operation may be undertaken by the Safety Investigation Authority (SIA) leading an investigation to locate and gather evidence which may establish the cause of the accident. The decision to conduct an underwater search is determined on a case-by-case basis and a search would only be carried out if it was considered safe and practical to do so. The aim of a search would be to determine the location of the wreckage and to undertake an underwater survey; wreckage would only be recovered if it was considered feasible and necessary in order to understand the cause of the accident.

Probable location of the wreckage

The AAIB established the most likely location for where the aircraft struck the surface of the sea by analysing radar data and the flight profile during the final minutes of the flight. The Ministry of Defence's Salvage and Marine Operations (SALMO) Project Team then factored in the depth of water and tidal flow to determine the primary area for the seabed search, which was an area of 4 nm^2 approximately 22 nm north-northwest of Guernsey.

Coordination of the seabed search

Through SALMO, the AAIB contracted a specialist survey vessel, the Geo Ocean III, to undertake an underwater survey of the seabed to try to locate and identify wreckage from the aircraft. The AAIB was aware that a separate, privately funded search was to be conducted and established close liaison with those involved to maximise the chance of locating any wreckage and to ensure a safe search operation. The privately contracted vessel was the FPV Morven.

The search was planned to be conducted in two phases. The first phase would be a survey of the seabed by both vessels using towed side-scan sonar to identify objects of interest. The second phase would be an examination of those objects when the tidal flow allowed[7] using the camera on a Remotely Operated Vehicle (ROV) deployed from the Geo Ocean III. To ensure safe separation between the vessels and towed sensors, and to maximise the efficiency of the search, the area was split into two parts and each vessel was allocated one part (Figure 5).

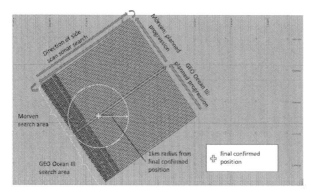

Figure 5

Seabed search strategy

Both vessels began their side-scan survey of the seabed on the morning of Sunday, 3 February 2019. Early in the search, the FPV Morven identified an object of interest at a depth of approximately 68 m and cleared the immediate area to allow the Geo Ocean III to launch its ROV and examine the object, which was identified as the missing aircraft. Figure 6 shows a side-scan sonar image taken from the Geo Ocean III.

An initial survey of the scene using the camera on the ROV revealed that there was a body present, held in place by the wreckage. The body was recovered to the vessel in the early hours of 6 February 2019 but, despite a further search of the wreckage and surroundings, no evidence was found of the second occupant of the aircraft. Shortly afterwards, a deterioration of the weather and sea conditions meant that it was not possible to safely continue the operation or recover the wreckage.

Footnote

[7] The search was made in an area of strong tidal flows which restricted the time the ROV could be deployed to periods of slack water.

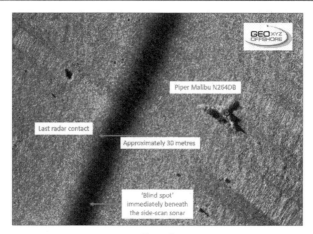

Figure 6

Side-scan sonar image of N264DB

Aircraft wreckage

ROV video footage

From the ROV video examination it was possible to establish that the aircraft was extensively damaged, and the main body of the aircraft was in three parts held together by electrical and flying control cables. The engine had disconnected from the cockpit area, and the rear section of the fuselage had broken away from the forward section adjacent to the trailing edge of the wing. The outboard section of both wings, tail plane and fin were missing. Figures 7 to 9 show images taken by the ROV.

Other wreckage

In the days following the accident two seat cushions, an arm rest and possible skin from the fuselage washed up along the coast of the Cotentin Peninsula, France. A seat cushion also washed up in Bonne Nuit Bay on the north coast of Jersey.

Figure 7
View looking at windscreen and cockpit area

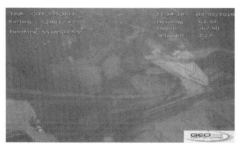

Figure 8
View looking at cabin and break in fuselage

Figure 9
View looking at remains of inner wing

Recorded information

Sources of recorded information

Recorded radar information (primary, and secondary Mode A and C[8]) was available from separate ground-based sites in Guernsey, Jersey and France. The radar data provided an almost complete record of the accident flight, starting as the aircraft took off and ending shortly before it struck the sea. The radar tracks from the different sites predominantly aligned, corroborating the relative accuracy of the independent data sources.

Recordings of RTF communications between the pilot and ATC were available and included the last radio transmission.

The pilot used a flight planning and navigation software application installed on his portable tablet computer to create a route between Nantes and Cardiff and file the VFR flight plan. This information had been uploaded to the pilot's cloud account[9]. During flight the tablet computer displays the aircraft position and planned route overlaid on a moving map, and records GPS-derived position information. The pilot's tablet computer was not found within the wreckage.

The aircraft was not fitted with an accident-protected flight data recorder or cockpit voice recorder and was not required to be.

Information from the recorded data

All times are UTC, and altitude is derived from Mode C data (transmitted in 100 ft increments with a tolerance of ±50 ft), corrected for local atmospheric pressure (QNH)[10].

After departure from Nantes, N264DB climbed progressively to 5,500 ft and its average ground speed was about 170 kt, equivalent to an estimated airspeed of 169 kt TAS based on a calculated wind from 250° at 25 kt. When the aircraft was about 20 nm south of Jersey, the pilot was transferred to the Jersey Control frequency.

On initial contact with Jersey ATC, the aircraft was cleared to enter controlled airspace and maintain FL55[11], following which the pilot was asked to advise ATC if at any time he would not be able to "MAINTAIN VMC"; this was to enable ATC coordination with other aircraft in the area should it be necessary for N264DB to descend or climb. At 1958 hrs, the controller asked the pilot to check if the aircraft's altimeter pressure setting was correctly set to 1013 hPa, because the information on the radar indicated FL53. The pilot acknowledged

Footnote

[8] Mode A refers to the four-digit 'squawk' code set on the transponder, and Mode C refers to the aircraft's pressure altitude which is transmitted in 100 ft increments. Secondary radar typically provides greater accuracy than primary radar.

[9] Cloud account refers to storage of data which is hosted remotely and made available to a user over a network (typically the Internet).

[10] Transmitted Mode C values are based on a standard pressure setting (see next footnote). This report has adjusted those values to reflect the local atmospheric pressure (QNH) so that they indicate altitude ie the vertical distance above mean sea level.

[11] Flight Levels (FL) are referenced to the International Standard Atmosphere (ISA) setting of 1013 hPa. FL55 is equivalent to 5,500 ft based on the standard pressure setting.

10

and, shortly afterwards, the aircraft climbed to FL55; the aircraft was about 11 nm south-west of Jersey.

At 2002:10 hrs, N264DB was about 11 nm west of Jersey and 13 nm south of Guernsey when the pilot requested clearance to descend to "MAINTAIN VMC" (Figure 3). The aircraft was cleared to FL50, with the instruction to advise ATC if a further descent was required. Shortly afterwards, the aircraft began to descend whilst also making a right turn followed by a left turn. This positioned the aircraft overhead Guernsey, about 1.5 nm parallel to the planned track. The controller then inquired if N264DB required a further descent, to which the pilot responded: "NEGATIVE, JUST AVOIDED A PATCH THERE, BUT BACK ON HEADING FIVE THOUSAND FEET".

At 2012 hrs, N264DB was about 11 nm north of Guernsey when the pilot requested a further descent to maintain VMC. The aircraft was cleared to descend at the pilot's discretion, and the pilot was given the Jersey QNH, which was 1017 hPa. The pilot acknowledged, and this was the last radio communication received from N264DB.

N264DB started to descend gradually and turned onto a track of about 060°T (Figure 10). Approximately 30 seconds later the aircraft turned left onto about 305°T. During this sequence of turns the aircraft descended from about 4,800 ft to 4,300 ft, climbed to about 5,000 ft, and then descended again to about 3,900 ft. The aircraft then proceeded to climb to about 4,200 ft on a track that was nearly parallel with the planned course of 343°T. Its average groundspeed was about 175 kt.

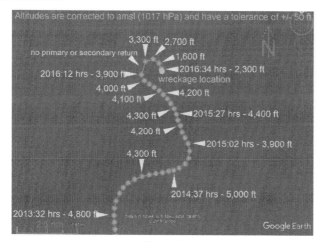

Figure 10

Radar track of final section of flight
(created from a combination of data from Jersey (Les Platons) and Guernsey radars)

11

At about 2015:30 hrs, N264DB started to make a gradual left turn, which was followed at about 2016:10 hrs by a right turn of approximately 180°. During this turn, data from two independent radars (Guernsey and Jersey[12]) showed the aircraft descend to an altitude of about 1,600 ft at an average rate of approximately 7,000 ft/min. A few seconds later (at 2016:34 hrs) the final secondary radar return was recorded, which indicated that the aircraft may have climbed rapidly to about 2,300 ft. Two more primary radar returns were recorded, timed at 2016:38 hrs and 2016:50 hrs respectively, but it is not yet known whether they represent valid returns from the aircraft.

The regulatory framework for the accident flight

The investigation is considering the regulations applicable to the operation of this flight including airworthiness requirements; flight crew licencing; and the carriage of passengers. The requirements are set out below.

Airworthiness, aircraft permissions and maintenance

Aviation in the USA is regulated by the FAA. The Code of Federal Regulations (CFR) Title 14 Aeronautics and Space (known as 14 CFR) contains the Federal Aviation Regulations and is available through the FAA website[13]. Any aircraft registered in the USA, wherever it is based in the world, is regulated in accordance with the FAA 14 CFR.

N264DB was subject to the requirements of FAR Part 91, *General Operating and Flight Rules*. These regulations allowed the aircraft to be flown by private pilots holding an appropriate licence, but it was not allowed to be used for commercial operations without the owner or operator first obtaining permission from the FAA and the UK Civil Aviation Authority (CAA).

Ownership of N264DB had been transferred into a US Citizen Corporate Trust (known by the FAA as the Trustee and the CAA as the Owner Trust), which was a requirement to allow it to operate on the US register. The Trustee had a written contract with a UK Company, the Trustor, which had originally purchased the aircraft before transferring the title deed to the Trustee on 7 August 2015. The Trustee was responsible for registering the aircraft and passing all applicable airworthiness directives to the Trustor (which is known by the CAA as the Beneficial Owner).

The Trustor was responsible for the operation of the aircraft, ensuring it was maintained in accordance with applicable regulations and met all airworthiness requirements. The Trustor had an informal arrangement with a third party to manage the aircraft on its behalf.

Neither the Trustee nor the Trustor had applied to the FAA or the CAA to operate the aircraft for commercial reasons. The CAA advised the AAIB that they had no record of an application for permission to operate the aircraft commercially.

Footnote

[12] Data points were recorded once every four seconds by the radar located at Guernsey and once every five seconds for the radar located at Jersey (Les Platons).

[13] https://www.faa.gov/regulations_policies/faa_regulations/ [accessed February 2019]

Oversight for the maintenance of aircraft operating in the UK which are registered in another State is carried out by, or on behalf of, the State of Registration, in this case the USA as represented by the FAA. The CAA may be asked to assist the FAA with safety checks or where a safety concern has been identified relating to a US registered aircraft operating in the UK.

Flight crew licencing

To fly an aircraft registered in the USA a pilot must hold a suitable licence, and licencing is governed by FAR Part 61, *Certification: Pilots, Flight Instructors, and Ground Instructors*. Part 61.3(a)(vii) states:

> *'When operating an aircraft within a foreign country, a pilot license issued by that country may be used.'*

Aviation in the European Union (EU) is regulated by the European Aviation Safety Agency (EASA), but pilot licences issued in accordance with EASA regulations are issued by Member State National Aviation Authorities (the CAA in the UK). A pilot may only hold one EASA licence, issued by a single Member State. The USA does not consider the European Union to be a State and so a flight between two EU Member States is a flight between two foreign countries within the meaning of Part 61.3(a)(vii). Such a flight would require the pilot to hold a licence issued in each Member State, which is not possible in the EU. Therefore, when an EASA licence issued in an EU Member State is used to fly an aircraft registered in the USA, the flight must remain within the borders of that Member State. The corollary is that, to fly an aircraft registered in the USA between two EU Member States, as was the case with the accident flight, a pilot must use an FAA licence.

Part 61 offers two routes to gain an FAA PPL and the first is laid out in Part 61.103. An FAA PPL would be gained this way by completing the FAA syllabus, examinations, flight training and flight test. Such a licence includes a night flying qualification because night flying is part of the FAA PPL syllabus.

The second way to gain an FAA PPL is through a certificate issued on the basis of a foreign pilot licence ('piggybacking'). The rules for this are contained in Part 61.75 which state that such a certificate:

> *'Is subject to the limitations and restrictions on the person's U.S. certificate and foreign pilot license when exercising the privileges of that U.S. pilot certificate in an aircraft of U.S. registry operating within or outside the United States.'*

It is possible for aircraft ratings and instrument ratings to be piggybacked onto an FAA licence from a foreign licence. For example, an FAA PPL issued on the basis of an EASA PPL could be used for night flying if the pilot had an EASA night rating (night flying is not included in the EASA PPL syllabus).

The pilot of N264DB held an EASA PPL, issued by the CAA in the UK, and an FAA PPL, issued on the basis of his EASA PPL. It is thought that the pilot's licence and logbook were lost with the aircraft and so the ratings on his licences and their validity, and the extent of his recent flying have not yet been determined.

Carriage of passengers

A PPL does not allow a pilot to carry passengers for reward; to do so requires a commercial licence[14]. The basis on which the passenger was being carried on N264DB has not yet been established but, previously, the pilot had carried passengers on the basis of 'cost sharing'. Cost sharing allows a private pilot to carry passengers and for those passengers to contribute towards the actual cost of the flight. Cost sharing brings benefits to private pilots who, by sharing the expense of their flying, can fly more than they might otherwise be able to, thereby increasing their level of experience. A higher level of regulatory burden applies to commercial, compared with private flights (such as more stringent medical, licencing and airworthiness requirements), and the additional requirements increase the level of safety assurance. Therefore, although the UK, EU and US regulatory authorities allow cost sharing, they apply restrictions to it.

European and UK national regulations permit pilots to share the direct costs of a flight without having to comply with regulations applicable to Commercial Air Transport or Public Transport flights. The proportion of the costs that must be shared by the pilot is not specified; however, the pilot must contribute to the actual direct costs of the flight being conducted. The CAA has produced guidance documents for the General Aviation community such as CAP1590, *Cost sharing flights: guidance and information,*[15] and CAP 1589, *Cost sharing flights: GA Guide*[16].

The EASA permits cost sharing on aircraft registered in a third country, such as the USA, but the relevant EASA rules state there may also be a requirement to comply with any regulations of the State of Registry. FAR Part 61.113 prohibits holders of a PPL from acting as Pilot in Command (PIC) of an aircraft carrying passengers for compensation or hire except in certain circumstances. When carrying passengers under the relevant dispensation a private pilot:

'may not pay less than the pro rata share of the operating expenses.'

Footnote

[14] Commercial Pilots Licence (CPL) or Airline Transport Pilots Licence (ATPL).
[15] CAP 1590. Available: https://publicapps.caa.co.uk/docs/33/CAP1590%20Cost%20Sharing%20Flights%20 (Aug%202018).pdf [accessed February 2019]
[16] CAP 1589. Available: http://publicapps.caa.co.uk/docs/33/CAP1589%20-%20cost%20sharing%20GA%20 guide_v3%20(Aug%202018).pdf [accessed February 2019]

The FAA issued legal interpretations in 2009[17] and 2014[18] making clear that a pilot must not pay less than the pro rata share for the flight. If the flight involves the pilot and one passenger, then the pilot must pay half the operating expenses. The ruling also made clear that the pilot must have a bona fide purpose (also known as common purpose) for making the flight and must dictate when the flight is to go. The flight must not be made for the purpose of merely transporting the passenger.

Summary of regulatory issues

N264DB was registered in the USA and could not be used for commercial operations without permission from the FAA and CAA. At the time of writing there was no evidence that such permission had been sought or granted.

To fly an aircraft registered in the USA between EASA Member States, a pilot must operate using the privileges of an FAA licence. This licence may be:

a. Issued based on the privileges of an existing EASA PPL. If the EASA PPL contains a night rating, the FAA PPL will have night flying privileges.

b. Issued by the FAA following the completion of an approved PPL course. The privileges of a licence gained in this way will include night flying.

The pilot had an FAA PPL issued on the basis of his EASA PPL. His logbook and licence were not recovered from the aircraft, and the ratings on his licences and their validity dates have not yet been established.

If the flight was planned to be operated on a cost sharing basis, FAA rules regarding pro rata costs and a common purpose were applicable.

Further work

The investigation continues to examine all pertinent operational, technical, organisational and human factors which might have contributed to the accident. In particular, work will be undertaken to:

a. Refine the analysis of the radar information to try and understand the last few minutes of the flight.

b. Assess the possible implications of the weather conditions in the area at the time of the accident.

Footnote

[17] https://www.faa.gov/about/office_org/headquarters_offices/agc/practice_areas/regulations/interpretations/data/interps/2009/mangiamele%20-%20(2009)%20legal%20interpretation.pdf [accessed February 2019]

[18] https://www.faa.gov/about/office_org/headquarters_offices/agc/practice_areas/regulations/interpretations/data/interps/2014/macpherson-jonesday%20-%20(2014)%20legal%20interpretation.pdf [accessed February 2019]

    c.   Analyse video from the ROV to determine the aircraft attitude as it entered the water.

    d.   Consider the regulatory requirements surrounding the flight including airworthiness requirements, aircraft permissions and flight crew licencing.

A final report will be published in due course.

Published 25 February 2019

with applicable regulations and met all airworthiness requirements. A third party managed the aircraft.

The vehement denial by Willie McKay that he owned the fateful aircraft which carried Emiliano Sala led to a search for its owners. Investigations proved more complicated than anticipated and revealed the labyrinthine ways in which ownership appeared to be removed or withheld from the United States' Federal Aviation Administration in an attempt to keep the true owner's identity a secret. The Piper Malibu was registered in the US in the name of a British-based trustee firm, Southern Aircraft Consultancy Inc. The 35-year-old aircraft's listing with the US Federal Aviation Administration states that there were no previous owners, though that didn't prove to be the case.

Enquiries about the ownership of the plane at the time of the crash centred on a firm called Cool Flourish, listed at Companies House as a management consultancy business. All three past and present directors had UK addresses; two of those were empty, with all furniture removed, when the *Mail on Sunday* visited. The company's major shareholder, 45-year-old Fay Keely, is listed by the companies register as resident at a property at Alfreton, Derbyshire, which was deserted and unfurnished. Attempts by the newspaper to ask another director, Heather Keely, 41, about the business also drew a blank. A woman who answered the door of a listed address in Repton, Nottinghamshire, slammed it shut and refused to answer questions. A note requesting clarification went unanswered. A mansion listed as the home of an older former director Terence Keely was also empty. The *Mail on Sunday* were told that they were trespassing and must leave the premises by ground staff.

Evidence that McKay part-owned the plane or was linked to a commercial entity that did, which he denies, could be used by Cardiff to strengthen their case for negligence against Nantes, as McKay's son Mark had a mandate from the French club, and both the McKays were working for Nantes. Cardiff would argue that McKay was a representative of the French club, who therefore carry liability.

The FAA listed the craft as having been first flown in 1984. A 65-year-old pilot, Eduardo Hernandez Vidaurreta, from Burgos in northern Spain, told Spain's *El Pais* newspaper that he had owned the aircraft between 2012 and 2015 before he sold it to a buyer represented by the British-based Southern Aircraft Consultancy, who register planes for owners wanting to remain anonymous. During the sale Vidaurreta met David Henderson, the pilot who would use it to regularly fly Willie McKay's clients around the UK and Europe but did not take the controls on the night it crashed, instead passing the job onto his friend David Ibbotson. Vidauretta, an experienced pilot of over 40 years, told *El Pais* "It didn't give me any problems, if someone is looking for a mechanical reason to explain the airplane's crash, I think they are wrong." The Spaniard claimed the plane was "marvellous to fly" during the estimated 200 hours he piloted it between 2012 and 2015.

"The plane didn't fall to pieces, I'm sure it didn't," added Eduardo, a commercial pilot since 1976, who was hired to fly the light aircraft between 2012 and 2015 by his friend Roberto Sastre, a businessman from Valladolid who had bought the plane in 2012 for around 500,000 Euros. The plane, which originally belonged to an aviation school in Florida, had a new engine fitted when he brought it to Spain.

Sastre said the aircraft was in a "good condition" with life jackets and emergency oxygen tanks on board, when it was sold to the British company in 2015. "The company that bought the plane and sent a mechanic to Spain to inspect it," Sastre said, "They didn't find anything important. The plane could be sold, it was in good condition."

The plane appeared to have changed hands four times in a single day in 2015. The AAIB report states "the Trustor (Cool Flourish) had an informal arrangement with a third party to manage the aircraft on its behalf."

In October, 2015, one month after Cool Flourish bought

the plane from Clasik Allquiler De Clasicos S.L, Mr Henderson appeared in a BBC video feature in which he revealed he had brought the Piper Malibu N264DB aircraft "over from Spain a couple of weeks ago." The aircraft was based at Retford (Gamston) Airport, Nottinghamshire, at this time.

Henderson had declined to comment ever since the plane crash and it remained unclear exactly how Mr Ibbotson came to be flying the plane. The plane was not allowed to be used for commercial operations without permission from the Federal Aviation Administration (FAA) or UK Civil Aviation Authority (CAA). That permission had not been sought by the plane's owners or the Trustee company who hold the registration of the aircraft. The report does however state, "The basis on which the passenger was being carried on N264DB has not yet been established but, previously, the pilot had carried passengers on the basis of 'cost sharing'".

What the AAIB report says about the plane's ownership

Aviation in the USA is regulated by the FAA, and the US-registered Piper Malibu was subject to Federal Aviation Regulations, even though it was based in the UK.

These regulations allowed the aircraft to be flown by private pilots holding an appropriate licence, but it was not allowed to be used for commercial operations without the owner or operator first obtaining permission from the FAA and the UK Civil Aviation Authority (CAA).

Ownership of N264DB had been transferred into a US Citizen Corporate Trust (known by the FAA as the Trustee and the CAA as the Owner Trust), which was a requirement to allow it to operate on the US register.

The Trustee had a written contract with a UK Company, the Trustor, which had originally purchased the aircraft before transferring the title deed to the Trustee on 7 August 2015. The Trustee was responsible for registering the aircraft and passing all applicable airworthiness directives to the Trustor (which is known by the CAA as the Beneficial Owner).

The Trustor was responsible for the operation of the aircraft, ensuring it was maintained in accordance with applicable regulations and met all airworthiness requirements.

The Trustor had an informal arrangement with a third party to manage the aircraft on its behalf.

Neither the Trustee nor the Trustor had applied to the FAA or the CAA to operate the aircraft for commercial reasons. The CAA advised the AAIB that they had no record of an application for permission to operate the aircraft commercially.

How the plane's ownership changed hands

On September 11, 2015, the following sales documents were processed by the FAA in Oklahoma City. They show the plane effectively changing hands several times on the same day.

- Clasik, Allquiler De Clasicos S.L purchase the aircraft rights from Southern Aircraft Consultancy (SAC). They had previously sold the rights to SAC shortly after purchasing the aircraft in November, 2011.

- Cool Flourish buy the plane from Clasik, Allquiler De Clasicos S.L

- Cool Flourish sell and transfer the rights of the Piper Malibu to SAC

9: THE TWO FACES OF WILLIE McKAY

UNDER PRESSURE WILLIE McKAY IS ALLEGED to have issued death threats to four of Cardiff City's hierarchy in American Airlines' business lounge at Buenos Aires Airport on the return journey from Emiliano Sala's funeral but after a period during which he presented a public face claiming he was the victim, including interviews with the *Telegraph* and BBC News, he soon returned to pursuing a vendetta of his own against Cardiff City and anyone connected with them and members of the media including yours truly!

The Glaswegian former bookmaker turned football agent refused to discuss Cardiff's accusation that he had artificially inflated Sala's price when he was contacted by the *Daily Mail*. McKay repeatedly shouted "You're calling yourself a journalist are you?" at a reporter before saying "What are you calling yourself?" before putting down the phone. A second call elicited the same response. *The Times* newspaper came under siege from McKay when they published a story online that he owned the ill-fated plane. *The Times* had to apologise to McKay for the incorrect statement.

Such was McKay's anger that when *Telegraph* investigative journalist Ben Rumsby called McKay to discuss his involvement in Sala's fatal flight, the Scot sought to demand the newspaper publish an article highlighting *The Times* error. Another journalist recorded a particularly intimidating rant from McKay, but has requested not to be named in this book. The Scot shouted at him, "Where are you? Where are you? Tell me where you are?" The journalist asked McKay if he was threatening him. "No, I'm not threatening you" asserted the Scot but to the journalist on the end of the rant, it certainly felt as though he was!

However the *Telegraph* was far from alone in feeling the McKay pressure. Neil Ashton, *The Sun*'s Chief football reporter and host of Sky TV's Sunday Supplement, illustrated the way in which the Scot had tried to 'persuade' him of his case with a late night phone call. "When [Willie] McKay's name comes up on your phone shortly after midnight, as it did on mine on Wednesday, it is highly unlikely to be for a chat about the missed chance in the Liverpool-Bayern game," Ashton wrote in his *Sun* column on 21st February, "this time he was conciliatory, reasoned and, by McKay's standards, measured. In a conversation that lasted one hour and two minutes, McKay stressed that if his days making a mint out of the football business are over, then he will be taking a few people with him. He says he is prepared to take any question and has a few of his own he would like to ask."

The Scot was pushing for a Sky TV showdown between himself and the Cardiff City hierarchy where he could answer their questions about the transfer and subsequent tragedy and fire back with some questions of his own. Needless to say such a confrontation was out of the question, yet it showed McKay's frame of mind as he desperately sought to clear his name.

Cardiff owner Vincent Tan's stance against Willie McKay remains consistent with previous legal charges he has made against football agents. In December 2016 Cardiff lodged a claim of dishonest conspiracy against former manager Malky Mackay, former Director of Football Iain Moody and agents David Manasseh, Rob Segal and John Inglis. The civil case, in which Cardiff are claiming damages of £10m, remains lodged within the legal system.

A Ben Rumsby exclusive in the *Telegraph* at the end of June claimed that Willie McKay "has been charged with fraud and faced up to two years in prison". The Scot was alleged to have committed "two counts of fraudulent transfer of property" and was due in court over the charges. "If found guilty, Mr McKay faced up to two years in prison", the *Telegraph* reported.

In a statement by way of reply McKay said: "I wish to make it clear that contrary to the impression given in the media that I have been charged with property fraud, the fact is that I have been summonsed by the Insolvency service in the magistrates court on an allegation that I bought a watch and a car when I knew I was going to be adjudicated bankrupt. I will be vigorously defending these proceedings."

McKay wasn't happy again with the *Telegraph* or indeed Ben Rumsby when he was in court to deny two charges under the Insolvency Act, as the case was referred to Manchester Crown Court for a date in October. The charges are that as a bankrupt he made a gift of property by spending £9,100 to buy a Rolex Date Just II watch for his wife in Leeds on December 14 2014; and that a day later he spent £54,000 on a Jaguar XK5 car for his wife in Doncaster. McKay is said to have bought the items before Christmas 2014, when prosecutors allege he owed £902,000 to HMRC in unpaid tax and interest. They claim he had been notified of this in June 2014 and of bankruptcy in April that following year but the purchases were made before the money became part of the bankruptcy.

After entering his not guilty pleas the ten-minute hearing was adjourned for a pre-trial hearing. Outside court, McKay approached reporters and protested his innocence saying "This is an ongoing persecution. That's what this is all about." He claimed to be victim of a 'witch hunt' by the authorities after being asked whether this was the case by a reporter. Earlier Andrew Evans, prosecuting, said the gifts amounted to £63,100 and the matter should not be dealt with at the magistrates' court but at a higher court. David Marsh, defending McKay, said the defendant would elect to be tried by a jury at the higher court. McKay was given unconditional bail until his next appearance at Manchester Crown Court on October 3.

McKay's Bankruptcy Restriction Undertaking was for a period of five years, ending on 28 August 2023. The undertaking was signed by William McKay on 29 August 2018, having previously been explained the exact nature of the document by the Insolvency Service.

- A BRU forbids an individual from:
- Acting as a director of a company, or form, manage or promote a company, without permission from the court.
- Carrying on business under a different name without telling

people you do business with the name (or trading style) in which you were made bankrupt.

- Trying to borrow more than £500 without saying you are subject to restrictions.
- Being a trustee of a charity.
- Working in various posts in education such as being a school governor.

The Bankruptcy Order was made against Mr McKay on 30 March 2015 with unsecured liabilities of £5,679,746 and he was discharged from bankruptcy on 29 August 2018. Between June 2014, when HMRC asked for payments of £902,128, and 30 March 2015 when the Bankruptcy Order was made against Mr McKay, he disposed of £2,079,790 to the detriment of HMRC and became insolvent as a result.

The disposal of circa £2,079,790, included more than £610,000 spent on gambling, more than £420,000 withdrawn in cash and close to £100,000 spent on hotels, restaurants and entertaining expenses.

McKay, 60, of Craighead Road, Glasgow, then appeared at Leeds Crown Court on October 15 accused of two counts of fraud under the Insolvency Act. McKay denied the charges. The court heard the details of the charges as McKay appeared in the dock wearing a navy suit and navy and white striped tie and spoke only to enter his not guilty pleas and to confirm his name, date of birth and nationality as Scottish. Addressing the defendant, Judge Andrew Stubbs QC said, "I understand your defence is a straightforward one, that you accept what the prosecution say you did but you were not doing anything wrong." Kerrie Ann Rowan, defending McKay, said the defence had made an application to have the case transferred from Leeds to a London court. Judge Stubbs said he was unable to deal with the application and another judge would decide if a transfer was appropriate. He said, "This is the only hearing there will be before your trial, which, at the moment, is listed here on September 14. I know there is an application to move that case, that's not a decision I can make today." McKay remains on bail pending trial at the time this book went to press.

The Two Faces of Willie McKay

Mercato Sports - registered in the names of Mark McKay and Janie McKay, the wife of his businessman father Willie McKay - appeared at the High Court in London to face an application from HM Revenue and Customs to wind up the company. A barrister for HMRC told the court "The debt has been paid. The petition is dismissed with costs." The amount of debt owed was not mentioned in court. Businesses can be issued with the notice and forced to liquidate all of its assets if it fails to repay a debt of more than £750 within 21 days of being asked for it. The company is one of four that represented Sala.

Working with Ben Rumsby was a pleasure, he is a meticulous journalist of immense integrity. However when it eventually dawned on Willie McKay that I was working alongside him (which wasn't hard to detect as my by-line was frequently used!) I was accused of waging a vendetta on the Scot. I worked for the *Telegraph* on background, using my contacts to dig up information surrounding the football side of the transfer and was never directly employed by the newspaper and Ben wrote each article, I couldn't have mounted a vendetta even if I had wanted to!

Ben had maintained a reasonable relationship with McKay. Well, at least the Scot sometimes took his calls, but generally ignored any correspondence when being given the right of reply. Ben told me that his relationship had been good up until the time that McKay suddenly discovered that I had been contributing to the *Telegraph* articles! It was a mystery how it had taken him so long before he noticed. One can only imagine that one of his media contacts tipped him off perhaps.

Kendall Street in Bayswater is one of the more affluent areas of London. One day in February, someone closely linked to Cardiff

City left his affluent home for a coffee break and headed to the nearby Le Pain Quotidien, one of those up market cafés renowned for artisan lattes and frothy cappuccinos - a venue ideal for a time of quiet reflection during lunch. Set back off the Edgware Road, just behind Marble Arch tube station, north of Hyde Park, this was a sanctuary of peace and solitude with a few tables and chairs outside for the well-heeled clientele offering the chance to unwind from the bustle of central London, or rather it is supposed to be...

Suddenly the victim, who asked not to be named as he was terrified of any further recriminations, was rudely interrupted by the unannounced appearance of a formidable figure in the shape of former Glaswegian bookie Willie McKay who was anxious for a face-to-face confrontation just six days after Emiliano Sala's funeral. The victim had already received intimidating telephone calls from the Scot who made his feelings pretty clear about how Cardiff City had "thrown me under the bus" and how he felt that false stories circulating about him might impact on his kids; his twin boys who were making a start in their professional football career, and his son Mark, who was hoping to follow his father into business as a football agent.

It was already well known within the Welsh club's upper echelons, and their lawyers at Capital Law, that McKay was on the rampage issuing all sort of vile threats, taken so seriously that statements had been taken via the club's lawyers from all of McKay's victims, and the South Wales Police had been alerted.

It transpired that in the days before he caught up with his victim, Chris Nott of Capital Law had a call from an irate McKay recorded for posterity on voice-mail during which the Scot ranted that he wanted to know where he could find him. "Where is he? I'm going to get him!" McKay warned. In the end he clearly didn't need Nott's help in locating him!

McKay's latest victim was sure the Scot had been "stalking him" before accosting him outside the coffee shop close to his home and had followed him when he left his house. That would have been the main thrust of his witness statement to Metropolitan Police plus the tone and threats issued by McKay as it didn't take long before the Scot's frustrations boiled over. According to his victim, the encounter with McKay ended with the Scot mentioning he still knew some gangsters in his home town of Glasgow where his parents lived, saying "You don't know who you're f★★★★★★ dealing with!" The victim's statement was one of four taken down by Capital Law in connection to McKay's threats. As this incident took place in London the incident was passed on by South Wales Police to the Metropolitan Police. The Met investigated a "possible public order offence" without giving any details to whom it referred.

In complete contrast, just days later McKay and his son Mark looked grief-stricken and anguished when answering Dan Roan's questions before BBC News cameras in his lavish Doncaster home, claiming he "didn't care if Nantes pay us".

Allegations of death threats to Cardiff City executives had first been revealed in the *Sunday Telegraph*, which also disclosed how Cardiff City's manager Neil Warnock had witnessed, in part, one of the threats at the airport on the way back from Emiliano Sala's funeral. Warnock gave a witness statement to South Wales Police. When the alleged death threats first started lawyers from Capital Law wrote to McKay warning the Scot that the club might consider banning him form their ground and that he could "not bully a solution" and that they would, if need be, resort to the law to restrain him. The letter pointed out that there was no way that the club would agree to McKay's public baiting for a TV debate on the issues surrounding the Sala tragedy due to his unreasonable and aggressive behaviour.

McKay was not arrested and still denies any wrongdoing but it is clear that the Met investigated the Bayswater confrontation. A spokesperson for them said: "The Metropolitan Police Service received an allegation of a public order offence in Kendall Street, W2 on Friday, 22nd February. Officers from the Central Area Command Unit investigated. A man, aged in his 50s was interviewed under caution on Tuesday, 28th May. He was not arrested. The man was issued with a first instance harassment warning. The investigation has now concluded."

McKay denied being issued with a harassment warning by

police following complaints he committed a public order offence. He told journalists, including Ben Rumsby, that he had not received a warning from the Met. He also claimed that he had to be interviewed on a Tuesday because the Monday was a Bank Holiday and the police were reluctant to pay an officer double time.

Neil Warnock questioned by police investigating accusations Willie McKay threatened to 'kill everybody'

Ben Rumsby, Harry Harris

16 MARCH 2019

Neil Warnock has been questioned by police investigating accusations Willie McKay threatened to "kill everybody" at Cardiff City, the *Sunday Telegraph* can reveal.

It can be disclosed that Warnock witnessed one of the alleged altercations between the man who booked Emiliano Sala's doomed flight and senior club officials, which this newspaper exclusively revealed were being probed by South Wales Police.

Cardiff's manager has been interviewed having previously told the *Telegraph* he had not heard much of an exchange that formed part of a formal complaint to the police.

It can also be revealed that there are four people to whom such threats were allegedly made, both in person and over the telephone.

All four, who the *Telegraph* has agreed not to name, have been questioned as well by officers after providing them with formal witness statements.

As of last week, police had yet to interview McKay, who has already denied the accusations against him.

He also has a long history with Warnock, who told the *Telegraph* last month he had fallen victim to a "vendetta" over the pair's links since Sala's tragic death and denied they were "big pals".

Cardiff on Saturday declined to comment on what is an ongoing investigation, having previously said: "It was necessary and appropriate for South Wales Police to be engaged on the matter."

Among their accusations is that McKay threatened to "kill everybody" at the club on the same weekend as Sala's funeral in Argentina a month ago.

He is alleged to have told officials: "I'll kill everybody if my sons get slaughtered".

McKay's eldest son, Mark, was one of the agents involved in Sala's transfer from Nantes to Cardiff, while another of his sons, Jack, helped make arrangements for the player's doomed trip.

McKay has previously claimed he and his children, two of whom are Cardiff players, had "been through hell" over reprisals that followed the January 21 plane crash.

He has also accused Cardiff of "trying to throw me under the bus" and of attempting to shift blame for Sala's death on to "an easy target".

This *Telegraph* has been told his alleged threats prompted club lawyers to write to his lawyers requesting he desist and banning him from their stadium.

McKay has previously been abusive towards *Telegraph* reporters investigating the flight that killed Sala.

News of the police investigation followed an explosive television interview with McKay last month which cast major doubt on the legality of that flight.

In it, McKay admitted agreeing to pay the entire cost of the journey, a practice banned for such trips under the Civil Aviation Act.

That is because neither the pilot, Dave Ibbotson, nor the plane, a Piper Malibu PA-46-310P, had been licensed to undertake commercial flights.

McKay has repeatedly stated that Sala's fatal flight was booked via Dave Henderson, an experienced light-aircraft pilot who had flown him around Europe on many occasions, and that he had no input into the selection of pilot or plane.

Henderson has yet to comment on any of McKay's claims and attempts to reach him have been unsuccessful.

Metropolitan Police to Investigate Accusations Willie McKay threatened to 'kill everybody' at Cardiff City

Ben Rumsby, Harry Harris

20 MARCH 2019

A police investigation into accusations Willie McKay threatened to "kill everybody" at Cardiff City has been transferred to the Metropolitan Police, the *Daily Telegraph* can reveal. The country's biggest police force has become involved in an inquiry begun by South Wales Police following a complaint by the club over alleged threats made to senior officials by the man who booked Emiliano Sala's doomed flight.

The police investigation was exclusively revealed earlier this month by the *Telegraph*, which also disclosed this week that Cardiff manager Neil Warnock had been questioned by officers after witnessing one of the alleged altercations.

Confirming the switch of jurisdiction, South Wales Police said on Wednesday: "This investigation has been transferred to the Metropolitan Police Service."

The force indicated that the transfer had occurred because at least one of the alleged offences had taken place in the London area.

As revealed by the *Telegraph*, there are four people to whom threats were allegedly made, both in person and over the telephone.

All four, who this newspaper has agreed not to name, have been questioned as well by South Wales Police after providing it with formal witness statements.

Warnock has been interviewed having previously told the *Telegraph* he had not heard much of an exchange that formed part of a formal complaint to the police. As of last week, police had yet to question McKay, who has already denied the accusations against him.

The Met did not respond to requests for comment on Wednesday on its involvement in the investigation.

Cardiff City FC declined to comment, having previously said: "It was necessary and appropriate for South Wales Police to be engaged on the matter."

Among their accusations is that McKay threatened to "kill everybody" at the club on the same weekend as Sala's funeral in Argentina a month ago.

He is alleged to have told officials: "I'll kill everybody if my sons get slaughtered."

McKay's eldest son, Mark, was one of the agents involved in Sala's transfer from Nantes to Cardiff, while another of his sons, Jack, helped make arrangements for the player's doomed trip.

McKay has previously claimed he and his children, two of whom are Cardiff players,had "been through hell" over reprisals that followed the January 21 plane crash.

He has also accused Cardiff of "trying to throw me under the bus" and of attempting to shift blame for Sala's death on to "an easy target".

The *Telegraph* has been told his alleged threats prompted club lawyers to write to his lawyers requesting he desist and banning him from their stadium.

McKay has previously been abusive towards *Telegraph* reporters investigating the flight that killed Sala.

He also has a long history with Warnock, who told the *Telegraph* last month he had fallen victim to a "vendetta" over the pair's links since Sala's tragic death and denied they were "big pals".

News of the police investigation followed an explosive

television interview with McKay last month which cast major doubt on the legality of Sala's fatal flight.

In it, McKay admitted agreeing to pay the entire cost of the journey, a practise banned for such trips under the Civil Aviation Act.

That is because neither the pilot, Dave Ibbotson, nor the plane, a Piper Malibu PA-46-310P, had been licensed to undertake commercial flights.

McKay has repeatedly stated that Sala's fatal flight was booked via Dave Henderson, an experienced light-aircraft pilot who had flown him around Europe on many occasions and that he had no input into the selection of pilot or plane.

Henderson has yet to comment on any of McKay's claims and attempts to reach him have been unsuccessful.

Cardiff also backed calls on Tuesday for an investigation into other flights arranged by McKay as part of Sala's transfer after concerns were raised about their licensing by the Air Charter Association.

Meanwhile, FIFA had been given Cardiff until April 3 to respond to a complaint by Nantes over the Welsh club's refusal to pay the first instalment of Sala's transfer fee.

Cardiff are withholding the money pending the outcome of investigations into the player's death.

They said: "The club is aware of the FIFA request for a response and is processing that accordingly. We have no further comment on it at this stage."

The Two Faces of Willie McKay

Willie McKay allegedly threatened to 'burn' Cardiff City and warned "I'll shoot the lot of you"

Ben Rumsby and Harry Harris

23 MARCH 2019

Willie McKay threatened to "burn" Cardiff City and warned "I'll shoot the lot of you", according to a complaint that is now being investigated by the Metropolitan Police.

The *Sunday Telegraph* can reveal more of the threats Cardiff claim were made to, among others, senior club officials by the man who booked Emiliano Sala's doomed flight.

Three weeks after this newspaper disclosed police were investigating accusations McKay threatened to "kill everybody" at the Premier League side, it has also emerged he found out where one of the persons to whom threats were allegedly made lived before confronting him at a nearby café.

As revealed by *The Telegraph*, the Met launched an investigation into "a possible public order offence" close to one of his alleged threatened person's London homes.

The police said the alleged incident a month ago is "not being treated as 'threats to kill' and that no arrests have been made 'at this time'".

The Met confirmed it had launched an investigation 2½ weeks after South Wales Police said it had opened its own inquiry into a complaint by Cardiff about the man who also helped broker Sala's tragic transfer from Nantes.

That complaint included an accusation that he warned, "I'll burn Cardiff", during an angry phone call with a club official three weeks after Sala died in a plane crash in the English Channel.

It also claimed the alleged victim McKay confronted in person a month ago was subjected later that day to threatening calls in which the Scot said, "I'll shoot the lot of you" and, "You don't

147

know who you're dealing with".

The *Telegraph* previously revealed that McKay had been accused of saying, "I'll kill everybody if my sons get slaughtered", on the same weekend as Sala's funeral in Argentina last month. McKay's eldest son, Mark, was one of the agents involved in Sala's transfer from Nantes to Cardiff, while another of his sons, Jack, helped arrange the player's doomed trip.

It can now be disclosed the threat to "kill everybody" was allegedly issued to Cardiff chief executive Ken Choo and player-liaison officer Callum Davies in American Airlines's business lounge at Buenos Aires Airport.

As of last week, police had yet to interview McKay.

Having repeatedly ignored questions from this newspaper about his alleged threats to Cardiff officials, he granted an interview to *L'Equipe* yesterday in which he declined to comment on the Met investigation.

He did admit to an altercation with Choo at Buenos Aires Airport, comparing it to "a football match when two managers have an argument on the touchline".

But he denied threatening to kill everybody at the club and questioned why Cardiff had waited a fortnight to involve the police if they believed he had done so.

Cardiff declined to comment.

The Two Faces of Willie McKay

Willie McKay's 'threat' to 'burn' Cardiff City and 'kill everybody there' prompts police issue harassment warning

Ben Rumsby Harry Harris

25 JUNE 2019

Police issued a harassment warning to Willie McKay following a complaint that he threatened to "burn" Cardiff City and to "kill everybody there", *Telegraph* Sport can reveal.

The man who booked Emiliano Sala's flight was interviewed under caution by the Metropolitan Police after being accused of making threats to Cardiff chairman Mehmet Dalman, chief executive Ken Choo, player liaison officer Callum Davies and one other man.

As revealed by The *Telegraph*, the Met launched an investigation after McKay, who turned 60 this month, found out where one of his alleged victims lived and confronted him at a nearby café before committing what the force described as a "possible public order offence".

The Met said the incident was not being treated as "threats to kill" amid claims the Scot subjected the same man later that day to threatening phone calls in which he said, "I'll shoot the lot of you" , and, "You don't know who you're dealing with."

Confirming its investigation into the Feb 22 altercation had "now concluded", the Met said: "A man, aged in his fifties, was interviewed under caution on Tuesday, May 28. He was not arrested. The man was issued with a first instance harassment warning."

The force issued a statement less than a week after the pilot McKay asked to organise Sala's fatal Jan 21 flight was arrested on suspicion of manslaughter by an unlawful act.

Dave Henderson, 64, was held by Dorset Police amid an investigation into the striker's death, including accusations the man drafted in to fly the plane, Dave Ibbotson, was not properly licensed.

McKay has repeatedly stated he had no input into the selection of Ibbotson, who is missing presumed dead, while Henderson has yet to comment on his own arrest or role in the tragedy.

South Wales Police and the Met launched separate investigations into McKay following a complaint by Cardiff about the man who also helped broker Sala's tragic transfer from Nantes.

That complaint included an accusation that he warned, "I'll burn Cardiff", during an angry phone call with Dalman three weeks after Sala died over the English Channel.

It also featured a claim McKay told Choo and Davies, "I'll kill everybody if my sons get slaughtered", while the trio were attending Sala's funeral in Argentina the following month.

McKay's eldest son, Mark, was one of the agents involved in Sala's record £15 million transfer from Nantes to Cardiff, while another of his sons, Jack, helped arrange the player's trip.

Bluebirds manager Neil Warnock was questioned by South Wales Police after witnessing the altercation at Buenos Aires Airport, having previously told The *Telegraph* "he had not heard much of what was said.

Cardiff declined to comment on McKay's harassment warning, having previously said it had been "necessary and appropriate" to engage the police on the matter.

McKay, who has repeatedly ignored questions from this newspaper in relation to Sala's death, did not respond to requests for comment before publication.

But he later denied any wrongdoing and said the police had not issued him with any harassment warning.

The Scot did admit to an altercation with Choo in an interview with *L'Equipe* in March, in which he compared it to "a football match when two managers have an argument on the touchline".

But he denied threatening to kill everybody at the club and questioned why Cardiff had waited a fortnight to involve the police if they believed he had done so.

10: KNIVES OUT FOR NEIL WARNOCK

NEIL WARNOCK SOON FOUND HIMSELF IN THE firing line due to his close working relationship with Willie McKay. In the aftermath of the crash you could excuse the Yorkshireman from wanting to distance himself from his old colleague due to the on-going conflict between his employers and a man he had always relied on to find promising transfer targets, particularly when McKay had a big foothold in France. However when it all went pear-shaped and the agent needed Warnock's help in trying to find a solution with Cardiff, he discovered that his old pal wasn't so forthcoming and a rift formed between the two.

It's clear that Warnock and McKay worked very closely on the Sala deal. There had been a reluctance at board level to pay the asking price for a player without Premier League experience. To the members of the transfer committee, Sala represented a huge risk; here was a record signing aged 28 who had done little of note in France until just a few months before. £15m was a lot of money, a club record fee, but on the other hand Neil Warnock had just led the Welsh club back into the promised land of the Premier League so still enjoyed considerable capital with the Cardiff board. Now, with their record signing dead, there was no way the club were willing to part with the agreed transfer fee while there remained so many unanswered questions, especially those surrounding the role of Warnock's old pal Willie McKay.

Cardiff wanted Warnock to keep his distance from McKay for obvious reasons. The Cardiff boss was told that any public utterances on the Sala case should be made through the club and the club's newly appointed PR company Mercury and George Tucker who was assigned the daunting prospect of presenting Cardiff's case to the media. McKay, naturally, wanted Warnock to publicly exonerate him and the straight-talking Yorkshireman couldn't serve two masters. However in the weeks following the crash the Cardiff boss found himself at the centre of accusations about how son's agency management company ended up on Cardiff's books. So while Warnock was embroiled in the decision to force through the signing of Sala over the opposition of the Cardiff chairman, as an employee of the club he was unable to publicly exonerate McKay while Cardiff were investigating as many aspects of the transfer as they could in order to delay payments to Nantes. In short, Warnock was snookered!

In February, *The Sun* reported: "Between February 1, 2017 and January 31, 2018, Unique Sports Management, the firm James Warnock works for, had a hand in six player transactions. The torch is being shone on Cardiff because of the Emiliano Sala transfer from Nantes." It emerged that James Warnock had brokered deals for Cardiff captain Sean Morrison's three-year contract with the club in summer 2017 and was also used to negotiate the deal for forward Rhys Healey, brought in when Craig Noone's contract with the Bluebirds was cancelled. The manager's son was also named on the paperwork for the final year of one of his dad's players at his old club QPR, Jamie Mackie.

USM had other players at Cardiff; Lee Peltier's contract was handled by Will Salthouse, one of the directors at USM, striker Lee Tomlin's move from Bristol City was handled by another USM employee, former Rochdale forward Clive Platt. Another USM employee helped to get a deal for Yanic Wildschut. Meanwhile the McKay's had done pretty well out of the Welsh club as well with Mark McKay representing Sol Bamba via his firm ExCel Foot and as late as January 2019 USM were used to complete the deal for Reading winger Leandro Bacuna on deadline day.

Section E4 of the FA rules entitled 'Working with Intermediaries Regulations' were updated in 2006 to ban members of a manager's family from being involved as agents in transfer deals. Ironically the law came about following a deal involving the Warnocks when Neil was manager of Sheffield United. As *The Guardian* said at the time, "The new regulations will extend the existing rules outlining 'conflicts of interests' to outlaw a repeat of the situation that has allowed David Unsworth, whose agent HN Sports employs James Warnock, the son of the Sheffield United manager Neil, to sign for that club." Of course the Warnocks are not the only family involved in what might be described as nepotism as the spotlight also fell on Alex Ferguson's son Jason being the agent of as many as 13 Manchester United players during his father's tenure at the Old Trafford club.

Then there is the question of Warnock's role in the signing of Willie McKay's twin sons. Prior to signing for Cardiff, the twins had followed their father around; signing for Doncaster Rovers, where Willie had an exclusive consultancy, and then Leeds United whose manager, Willie's fellow Scot Steve Evans, personally recommended the pair. Jack, a striker, made 4 goalless appearances for Doncaster and none for Leeds, while centre-half Paul made no appearances for Doncaster and one for Leeds (against Sutton in the FA Cup). Neither of the twins, now in their early 20s, got a first team appearance between them at Cardiff and they have since left the club - Jack signing for National League Chesterfield and Paul for Airdrieonians in Scotland.

My personal relationship with Neil Warnock goes back many years. I can recall him telling me that he suspended a training session at Crystal Palace when I telephoned the training ground asking to speak with him. Warnock claimed he'd told the assembled professionals "if the Chief Football Writer for the *Daily Mirror* is calling me, then it must be important!" All joking aside, I enjoyed a good working relationship with Neil and caught up with him whenever he was in London.

As a result I managed to acquire the first major interview with the Cardiff City manager at a time when he was being hounded in certain sections of the media for his son's connections with his current club and the allegation that this contravened FA rules. Behind the mask he wore for the cameras it has been far worse for the manager who had championed Sala as the answer to his team's lack of cutting edge in front of goal but then saw the deal end in tragedy.

"I have put on a front whenever the world's media gathered for press conferences, with such a global interest into what happened," he confessed, "I have never known anything like it, the emotional side of what has happened here, and it has affected me more than anything has ever affected me in football. You would have thought at my age, my time of life, I had seen it all, experienced it all. It's been bad, really bad behind the scenes. I think I have put up a good front in press conferences.

"It's been one thing facing the media at press conferences, but behind the scenes it has been far harder to take, and that's why I was crying on the pitch, because I saw my wife Sharon and the kids in the stands and it came over me. It has been terrible at home, the emotion of it all. I am sure everyone knows how I have also suffered for the last couple of years with Sharon's illness."

Sharon's battle with cancer and lymphoedema took its toll on Neil's home life, but as he was emerging from that debilitating experience, the shock of Sala's death, then the repercussions and insinuations that followed made life intolerable. Warnock added: "How can I not feel it, how can I not feel all the responsibility of it all. If I hadn't have gone for the player, he would still be here, I cannot stop thinking about our conversations, and especially the one just before we were heading off to Newcastle for a Premier League game and I asked him to come with us."

Speculation has intensified that Warnock's state of mind will inevitably result in him quitting Cardiff, maybe even football altogether but his answer to that point is sharp and to the point.

"No! It's just not true!" He snaps. "When I am asked the question I say it goes through my mind, well of course it would. At times like this who wouldn't feel like that? But I have a job to do, I want to fight on, I have no intention whatsoever of packing it in. It means, though, that you realise, if you didn't already, that there are far more important things in life than football, life itself. I never said I would pack in, never said that.

"Before the Arsenal game, if anything it made me more determined that I should do whatever I can to fight to keep Cardiff in the Premier League, even though we all already knew it would take a miracle to stay up, even before we lost the player whom I wanted, as I thought this striker would save us from going down."

Managers are always judged on results and results, more often than not, depend on the quality of player the manager can attract in the transfer market. For Warnock the January transfer window represented a chance to push the team towards safety. He had declined the usual agents' recommendations, which must have totally close to 50, to choose sale. Why a relatively unknown striker playing in the French league, ahead of so many other options; some cheaper, some more expensive and others with greater reputations and several with greater experience of playing in England?

"I went to watch him twice over there, I had seen him on a number of occasions. He had reached the stage in his career where he was ready to have a crack at the Premier League. He was comfortable in France, loved it in Nantes, but this was his time to test himself in English football. It was first suggested in the press that he didn't want to play for Cardiff, but when I asked him about that, he said that wasn't true. He did say that he wondered when it would be right time to go to the Premier League. What struck me most about him was that he was such a nice lad. Both times I saw him his clothes were really way out; he had holes in his jeans, and I said to him that he looked scruffy enough to fit in with us!

"He came over for his medical just before our game at Newcastle, so didn't train with us but I spent five minutes with him near our training ground, and asked him if he wanted to come to Newcastle. I also asked him 'Are you looking forward to playing for us?' He said he was but he wanted to go home to get some gear and to say goodbye to his team-mates. I was not aware of how he was getting to Nantes, no idea he was travelling in that plane, I was concentrating on our game at Newcastle as you'd expect."

It is Warnock's link to McKay that attracted the most scrutiny. Warnock feared it was the McKay connection that was being used against him. "Guilty before being proven innocent," Warnock says of the headlines and stories that emerged in the aftermath of the tragedy. "I have been involved with three players with Willie McKay in the last eight years. One of them has been a free transfer who has proved to be our star player and one of the best in the

Premier League, so you can't knock it? It's disgusting that a lot more has been suggested, but Cardiff have dealt with these agents long before I arrived at the club."

Warnock went on to tell me he considered there was a witch hunt going on and that there was a vendetta against him, and that made the big headlines in the *Sunday Telegraph* exclusive, and like all the *Telegraph* exclusives it was picked up just about everywhere around the world.

NEIL WARNOCK EXCLUSIVE:
"I've faced a vendetta over my links to 'Emiliano Sala agent'"

Tom Morgan, sports news correspondent and Harry Harris

9 FEBRUARY 2019

Neil Warnock says he has fallen victim to a "vendetta" over his links with the controversial businessman involved in the Emiliano Sala tragedy.

In his most candid interview since Sala was killed in a plane crash, Warnock claims he had no choice but to use Willie McKay's help in signing the striker from Nantes for £15 million. The Cardiff City manager told The *Sunday Telegraph* he had been "putting on a front" to give the impression he was coping with criticism and rumours around the disastrous deal.

"It's been bad, really bad behind the scenes," he said.

McKay, who unregistered with the Football Association, has faced scrutiny over his business dealings after he confirmed making the arrangements for Sala's doomed flight. The Monaco-based intermediary, who was declared bankrupt in 2015, has voluntarily disclosed details of how he muscled in on the Sala deal in January and planted fake stories to create a "buzz".

Warnock said of their relationship: "It's suggested I am big pals with Willie McKay. Am I? I don't think I am. He is an agent. You need these agents if you want to do a deal."

McKay's operation in bringing players from France to the Premier League is likely to eventually fall foul of tough new rules under consideration at FIFA, The *Telegraph* understands.

Greg Clarke, the FA chairman, refused to comment on the Sala case, but has confirmed he is working closely with FIFA on tougher curbs to ensure intermediaries are held to account. "I'm a big fan of making sure that the agents are regulated properly, and that the market is transparent and clean and conforms to best practice," he said. "I am sure most agents would want that too."

Clarke will have increasing influence after being elected this week as vice-president at FIFA, which is considering a 'clearing house' to scrutinise all transfers. The FA, he said, wants "sensible rules in place, drafted in conjunction with the players, FIFPro, the PFA and others that protect everybody. A transparent set of rules, a compliant set of rules, that is then adopted globally."

Warnock signed two of McKay's sons last year and had also used his services to sign Sol Bamba for free. The manager categorically denies the suggestion, however, that the Sala deal took place because of their relationship.

"I have been involved with three players with Willie McKay in the last eight years," he said. "One of them has been a free transfer who has proved to be our star player and one of the best in the Premier League, so you can't knock it. It's disgusting that a lot more has been suggested, but Cardiff have dealt with these agents long before I arrived at the club. Ask anyone in the game: if you want a player from France or a French player, 99 per cent of the time, you will have to deal with Willie McKay or someone like him. If you want to get the job done, then you need the Willie McKays of this world."

On 8th January - two weeks before the striker's death - McKay sent an email introducing himself to Sala, saying he would be able to get £1m for his mother if he signed for Cardiff. When approached by The *Telegraph* over the deal, McKay has been repeatedly abusive. Warnock said: "Someone suggested that if I went to Sala's funeral that Willie McKay would be standing alongside me. That was just distasteful."

The 70-year-old added: "There has been a vendetta in some quarters, of that I am sure, and our chairman has told me he doesn't want me to reply to them as it would destabilise the club."

Warnock, whose wife Sharon has been recovering after cancer treatment, said the timing of the tragedy has been particularly hard for his family. "It has been terrible at home, the emotion of it all," he said. "I am sure everyone knows how I have also suffered for the last couple of years with Sharon's illness."

As one might expect, Willie McKay did not like the article and he went to the media to ensure publication of his retribution. Whether McKay was behind it or not, the links with Warnock and his agent son and Cardiff were ramped up. *The Sun* followed by reporting that the FA wanted explanations about his son's involvement in three separate deals. The FA rulebook for agents, section E4, relates to a 'conflict of interest' surrounding deals that involve family members. But Cardiff told me that they had already notified the FA about the deals mentioned in the media, and told the game's ruling body that they were happy with the arrangement, aware that it might be construed as a conflict of interest. They expected that that would satisfy the FA enquiry.

Warnock was trying to keep Cardiff City in the Premier League and he had the backing of his chairman Mehmet Dalman and the Board. Dalman gave strong backing to Warnock over his connection with football agents saying, "I have absolutely no worries about that. We take our relationships from the day he started working at Cardiff. I don't really want to get involved in any vendettas and mud throwing. We have seen people taking knives out against Neil and that is just nonsense. I want to air my frustration with that behaviour and give my full support to what the team is doing. The best way to get even is by being successful. I am not going to pay attention to rumours and bad press. We just have to stay focused and do what we should be doing. That is to win football matches."

Dalman denied that his manager's close relations to McKay, although two of McKay's sons had been in the Cardiff Academy. "I feel the need to raise this," Dalman said. "I brought Neil into this club and I think he has done a tremendous job for us in more ways than one. It is important that he understands we are there for him. He was there for us in a difficult period and got us promoted. He has brought some great players into the club and I want him to know we are a family. The fans, the board, the chairman, the CEO and the owner are fully behind him as he strives to achieve the status of staying in the Premier League."

Dalman dismissed talk of Warnock stepping down after the manager said he considered his future "24 hours a day, seven days a week".

"That discussion has never taken place and I have absolutely no intention of holding that discussion," Dalman said.

At the end of the season Cardiff returned to the Championship, yet Neil Warnock received the support of Cardiff owner Vincent Tan to remain as the club's manager despite relegation.

Warnock seemed to question his own future after a 3-2 home defeat to Crystal Palace that confirmed Cardiff's return to the championship, the 70-year-old saying he had "no idea" whether he would be staying. But Malaysian businessman Tan delivered a vote of confidence and wanted Warnock to attempt to extend his own record of promotions as a manager to nine, telling BBC Sport Wales "I am happy for Neil to stay and achieve his ninth promotion."

Warnock had one season left on his Cardiff contract and would "let things settle" after the Palace defeat. Warnock has described the campaign, which concluded with a win at Manchester United, as the most difficult season of his 40-year managerial career.

Warnock was appointed Cardiff manager in October 2016 and took the Bluebirds up, a record eighth promotion. The Yorkshireman has worked on the smallest budget in the Premier League, but Cardiff's fate was not sealed until the penultimate game when they joined already-relegated Fulham and Huddersfield.

Warnock was given a rousing ovation at Cardiff City Stadium after the defeat by Palace, and afterwards goalkeeper Neil Etheridge said the players wanted him to stay. "His stats speak for themselves – eight promotions," Etheridge said. "He's a fantastic man-manager and knows exactly what to do."

11: THE CHAIRMAN

"He calls a mate who probably calls a mate, they find a plane but nobody seems to check the status of that plane. Is it licensed? Is it fit? The poor chap was colour blind. All the experts we interviewed said that any experienced pilot would have said no. I hold Nantes responsible for hiring an intermediary, a broker, and for allowing him to make the arrangements. As far as we are concerned he wasn't our player."

MEHMET DALMAN

IN THE AFTERMATH OF THE SALA TRAGEDY, Cardiff City's chairman Mehmet Dalman called for a radical regulation of football agents, likening the mentality of some to the Wild West. Dalman was particularly critical of Willie McKay, who was not a licensed agent yet was acting on behalf of his son Mark. Speaking at the FT Business of Football Summit in May, he launched a remarkable broadside into those he felt were responsible for the death of Emiliano Sala.

"It was shoddy behaviour, plain and simple. He [McKay] hides behind the licence of his son and we all think that's okay. He then calls a mate who probably calls a mate and then they find a plane and nobody seems to check the status of that plane. Is it licensed? Is it fit? Even Sala is leaving messages saying: 'I feel very unsafe in this thing'. It's clear the pilot shouldn't have been flying. The poor chap was colour blind. All the experts we interviewed said that any experienced pilot would have said no."

Dalman nodded when asked whether there was a 'Wild West' mentality in the world of agents. "The answer is yes," he said, "This is not just about McKay as there are many agents of that ilk in the industry". Dalman believed McKay "did the best that he thought he could do for the boy" in booking him on the doomed flight.

"Because it's how it's always been done, nobody questions it. So when we offered the British Airways flight to the player and he turned us down we assumed he had his own arrangements and it was no longer our concern. We made the offer and he declined. He didn't want to take the train because it would have taken longer and McKay's son stepped in and said 'don't worry about it, I'll get my dad to fix it'. I don't know Willie McKay at all. I've never met him and I don't particularly want to meet him. He acted in good intentions, but that doesn't make it right.

"He meant well. His intentions were good. But why do we have intermediary agents who are not transparent or accountable to anybody? That can't be right. Can you imagine any other industry where somebody is hiding behind somebody else's licence and gets away with it? When you speak to the old guard they say: 'I know, but we've always done things like this.' It doesn't make it right. We aren't punishing them. We need moves to be able to punish people for negligence.

"I'm from the City of London. My business is finance. Imagine we have a broker who has just been found guilty of whatever and he comes back as a broker hiding behind someone else's licence – there would be uproar. Why should football be any different? The whole intermediary issue needs to be dealt with."

Willie McKay played a central role in the transfer, despite falling foul of FA rules which disqualified anyone with bankruptcy orders from being registered intermediaries. Dalman says McKay should never have been involved in the deal. "First of all, I find it quite remarkable that he goes public and says 'I paid for the flight'. That makes it illegal: game, set and match. Secondly, he says 'I bumped up the price and I lied about other clubs being interested.' In the City of London, you go to prison. That is share price manipulation, yet we think it's okay and the guy keeps doing interviews. I don't think he means bad. He just doesn't know any different. There is a subtle difference."

The Cardiff chairman says he sometimes feels uneasy about the amounts being paid to agents from transfer deals. "I don't like it because the people who pay for it are the fans at the gate. So if you look at Sala and speculate for a second, he cost us £15m, that's public information. McKay has publicly indicated he was getting paid £1.5m and let's say Sala's agent was getting another million. That's £3m out of that £15m is going to agents, which fans are paying for. I think the regulators and the governing bodies need to do something about it. We had the big bang in 1987 and I think football now, the size of the industry we are in, needs a big bang. It needs a big bang in how it's governed because we are talking multi-billions and it's going to double, treble in the next three decades. We need to step up."

FIFA's proposals for transfer 'clearing houses' are a step in the right direction, he said, "but I would like to see more urgency about it. We aren't punishing them. We need moves to be able to punish people for negligence. I don't want to focus on McKay, but he works for Nantes, therefore it's the responsibility of Nantes, but where are they being held accountable for this... as far as I'm concerned, I hold Nantes responsible for hiring an intermediary, a broker, and for allowing him to make the arrangements."

Cardiff were still at an impasse with the French club over the transfer fee but Dalman insisted they were not looking to avoid their obligations. "We've never said we wouldn't pay. I have always said that we will do the right thing. But we want to know all the facts. There is a contractual disagreement between the two parties. As far as we are concerned he wasn't our player when this terrible tragedy happened, so in the letter of the law we are fine. However, we have taken a different approach and said: 'Look, this is a tragic event, it's a £15m dispute we are having here, isn't there a way where the two clubs can compromise and turn our attention to do something for the family?' Two months ago FIFA encouraged the clubs to get together and find a way forward. I have tried. But Nantes made it clear that they are not prepared to entertain that at the moment."

Dalman does not blame McKay or Nantes for the deal, but says: "We all have to take responsibility. We cannot take responsibility for what happened in the accident, but I just feel we should never have accepted the intermediary agent of this ilk. We need more regulation. I'm not saying we shouldn't have agents. Clearly they play a significant role in our industry, but it has to be regulated properly."

It has been a traumatic few months for Dalman who admitted that he initially opposed the deal after being quoted a £15m fee for Sala but was out-voted 3 to 1 by the other members of Cardiff's Transfer Committee made up of Chief Executive Ken Choo, senior director Steven Borley and manager Neil Warnock. After the initial tragedy of the events of January and the club's attempt to get on with a fight for survival in the Premier League, the threats made by Willie McKay to Cardiff officials which sparked police investigations in South Wales and London only added further stress to an already stressful situation for Dalman and the club.

Now Dalman has turned his attention to regulation of private flights to ensure a tragedy such as Sala's never happens again. He was lobbying the Government and Premier League to announce new laws to ensure athletes use only commercially-licensed aircraft, as he believes the sport should fall in line with the same safeguards that are in place in the financial sector. Cardiff joined forces with the British Air Charter Association (BACA) to demand "urgent action on illegal flights" and tougher punishments to protect all athletes from so-called "grey charters" defined as an unlicensed aircraft charter operation, meaning that the operator does not have a valid Air Operators Certificate (AOC) – generally, these are provided by private owners who do not need to adhere to the same regulations as an AOC holder, bypassing training, checking, oversight and compliance requirements which impact the layers of safety that a commercial operator provides. In Sala's case his plane was piloted by part-time gas engineer and DJ David Ibbotson who was colour blind and not licensed to take fee-paying passengers, across a dangerous stretch of water, the English Channel. It was an accident waiting to happen.

"This dreadful tragedy has highlighted that you can't sit still and do nothing any more. A 28-year-old boy lost his life because somebody didn't do proper due diligence. There is no regulation around it." Cardiff were putting in place robust checks and balances to ensure no more of their players or members of staff are endangered from such 'risky and illegal practices' again. They are calling on other clubs, and those in the horse-racing industry, where this practice is also common, to follow suit. Meanwhile Cardiff are in talks with Sala's family about setting up a trust fund.

Responding to Dalman's comments Willie McKay said: "Mehmet's a lovely man. He's been great for Cardiff City and my sons. Mehmet's going to do what he's going to do. I know he is under pressure from the owner." McKay said he had been acting in good faith by helping his son. He arranged the flight through the same man who had been helping him book flights for more than a decade.

In May Dave Edwards, chief executive of the Air Charter Association (BACA) commented, "The football season may be over, but the memories of 2018-19 will stay with fans for many years to come. There are some magical moments to remember - the Champions League semi-final comebacks, the thrilling title race, even Cardiff City's 2-0 win over Manchester United. But it was also a year of unprecedented tragedy.

"On the morning of January 22, reports began to filter in of a light aircraft missing over the English Channel. As the day went on it became clear that the missing Piper Malibu PA-46 plane was carrying Emiliano Sala, aged just 28, on his way to Cardiff from Nantes. Over the following days the footballing world watched, hoping for the best but fearing the worst. When his body was found, the world mourned.

"Amidst the collective trauma, it was not long before issues over the legality of the flight itself began to emerge. The Aviation Accidents Investigation Branch (AAIB) published an interim report on February 25 that confirmed what many suspected. Neither the pilot, nor the plane was licensed to operate on a commercial basis. The details that were revealed shocked many, but not the aviation industry, where it has long been said that it would take a high-profile accident before action would be taken to clamp down on the dangerous practice of illegal flying.

"Cardiff City FC are supporting the Air Charter Association in the hope that this tragic accident, might catalyse change. With the murky world of illegal flights having been uncovered for all to see, it is time to act.

"An illegal flight can take several different forms but as always, it ultimately comes down to pilots and flight organisers cutting corners. That can be by not attaining the proper licence to fly fee-paying passengers, by knowingly flying a plane that is not registered for commercial activities, or purposely flouting the cost sharing exemption (in which case a private pilot can fly up to six passengers if they are sharing the cost of the flight).

"It is important to make clear that the number of pilots who are happy to break the law are a small percentage of the 35,959 registered pilots in the UK. However, those who are breaking the law are breaking it often. There is circumstantial evidence to suggest illegal flights are happening every day at airfields around the country.

"After the Piper Malibu crash on January 21, the Air Charter Association launched a new reporting system for suspicious flights. Since then reports have come in at a rate of almost one per day. The prevalence of such flights lay solely at the door of those who have, for too long, been in a position to clamp down on illegal flights yet have chosen to look the other way.

"The past few months have highlighted that illegal flights are a real issue in the sporting world, most specifically the fast-moving football and horse racing industries. Football teams are regular users of private aviation and during transfer periods there is a boom in business.

"Meetings between agents, club officials and players are usually scheduled at short notice, in secrecy and under tight time pressures. Perhaps inevitably with the current culture of turning a blind eye, these flights are not always legal, and the Sala case, however shocking and tragic, is only the tip of the iceberg.

"While any recommendations for reform will come from the final Air Accidents Investigation Branch report due this year, there are actions we can take to stop others from needlessly taking risks. That is why we are helping the FA and Premier League to develop a new policy and are encouraging football clubs across the UK to adopt it as well.

"The policy has one very straightforward aim, to ensure that every flight connected to a football club is certified and that no player or member of staff is endangered through these risky and illegal practices again.

"It is essential that clubs institute robust checks and balances. Cardiff City FC is leading the way. We have hired an aviation expert who, before any flight takes off, will require a copy of the Air Operators Certificate, the Aircraft Insurance and evidence that all flight crew hold valid commercial pilot licences and all licences and certifications required for the plane to be flown.

"Only after the expert has given their thumbs up will the plane be cleared for take-off. And this process will and must extend to intermediaries with whom the club deals, only then will we make progress eliminating the practice of illegal flying from the football industry.

"This is an opportunity for those of us who are deeply troubled by what has happened to make real and lasting change in our industry."

12: FIRST ARRESTS AND CONVICTIONS

IN SEPTEMBER, A COURT HEARD THAT TWO people "driven by morbid curiosity" accessed CCTV footage of Emiliano Sala's post-mortem and shared images of it online. In the first of what could be a series of arrests and prosecutions connected to the case, the extent of the trauma, disgust and hurt felt by the footballer's family was expressed by his sister Romina who said the family were devastated after images leaked on to Instagram days after Emiliano's body was recovered.

CCTV firm manager Sherry Bray, 49, and her employee Christopher Ashford, 62, admitted illegally accessing mortuary footage of the striker's body. Judge Peter Crabtree jailed Bray for 14 months and Ashford for five months.

In a victim impact statement read to Swindon Crown Court during the sentencing hearing of Bray and Ashford, Romina said: "I cannot believe there are people so wicked and evil. I have seen photos of Emiliano's body leaked on Instagram. I phoned Emiliano's agent and told him what was circulating on the internet. I called our brother, Dario, and he did not want to see the photos. I tried to keep images off social networks. My mother could not see those horrible photos."

She said it was 'sad' because "People were making jokes about it. I'll never erase the images from my head. My brother and mother can never forget about this," she added. "It's hard for me to live with this image."

At Swindon Crown Court the judge said the offences were "driven by morbid curiosity" and in Ashford's case, "forensic science". The judge said they had taken place within "a culture" at the company where staff watched post-mortem examinations even though they "had no justification to do so".

Wiltshire Police started investigating when an image appearing to show Sala's body appeared on social media. On 18 February, officers investigated Camera Security Services in Chippenham, Wiltshire, and found the post-mortem test in Bournemouth had been viewed live on 7 February and then played back twice on 8 February.

After Sala's body was recovered from the plane, a post-mortem examination took place at Bournemouth Borough Mortuary the following day. The pair used their access to CCTV cameras at Bournemouth mortuary to grab images of his corpse on a phone. Bray, the director of Camera Security Services Limited in Chippenham, Wiltshire, and her employee Ashford, then accessed footage of the procedure being conducted on Sala. Bray sent it to a relative on Facebook and the horrific image of Sala's body was then shared around the world via social media. After realising that police were investigating, Bray deleted the file from her phone and asked Ashford to do the same but they were arrested and prosecuted with three counts of computer misuse.

Bray, of Corsham, and Ashford, of Calne, each admitted three counts of computer misuse in August. Bray also admitted perverting the course of justice by instructing Ashford to delete the images from the post-mortem cameras from the live feed camera facility, she also deleted the mortuary image of Sala from her phone.

Robert Welling, prosecuting, read to the court a text message exchange between Bray and Ashford at 14.26 on February 7 - while the footballer's autopsy was taking place. The first message, from Bray, read: "Nice one on table for you to watch when you are next in", followed by an emoji of a face being sick, Mr Welling said.

Ashford replied: "Not from the plane that crashed into the sea?"

He then sent a follow-up text which read: "Saw on the news this morning that body was being taken to Dorset, so guessed we might see it."

A later text exchange was also found between the two defendants, after Bray's daughter's boyfriend made her aware of the existence of the image online on February 12. A panicked Bray instructed Ashford to "delete your pics" before the two then discussed deleting CSS's live feed of the two autopsy room cameras.

Over the course of four police interviews, Bray admitted watching live footage of Sala's autopsy on February 7 and re-accessing it whilst on shift the following day. She said it was "just there" and that she had been "aware of the activity of police vehicles at the mortuary, and knew something big was going on," Mr Welling said.

When asked in interview whether she had the authority to watch it, she replied: "I have the authority to watch all the cameras, as long as I'm not abusing it - which I have done." She added: "I don't sit there watching mortuary footage all day, I'm not sick. Although I am sick, because I've just done that."

Bray initially admitted taking one photo, but then later owned up to the second image - but she insists she was not the one who shared the images online, stating that Twitter is "stupid".

She said that CSS is a company of approximately 20 people, and made clear that there were others "milling around" at the time the image was taken during Sala's autopsy.

In Ashford's police interview, Welling said that the 62-year-old "co-operated fully" and was "open and honest". Ashford, who had worked as a night-shift camera operative at CSS for 13 years, admitted that he had watched mortuary footage in the past, and had a "morbid obsession" with forensics.

Ashford admitted he had accessed parts of Sala's autopsy six times over three days, on February 9, 10, and 11, so he could watch it. He also told police he had taken one photo pre-autopsy, but said he deleted it prior to police involvement, "because he thought it was the wrong thing to do."

Welling told the court that it was clear that Bray had allowed a 'culture' to become embedded at CSS whereby she and other staff would watch autopsies 'as and when' on the mortuary CCTV footage.

Meanwhile, Richard Latcham - the son of Bray's other victim, Andrew Latcham - said the image Bray took of his father had cost him over £5,000 in counselling and lost earnings. Addressing Bray directly in his impact statement, he said: "Why would you do such a thing? This was such an unbelievably cruel and unnecessary act that bears no resemblance to the fabulous man my father was. Not for a minute did you stop to think about the impact your actions would have on the families of those you photographed."

Latcham told how his father took his own life in December 2017 after three months as a missing person, after being "tormented" by mental illness for a number of years. He said: "My dad was kind and considerate with a sharp intellect, and brought joy to his family with an anecdote, a wry smile, and an act of kindness. Sherry Bray's actions have created a distortion of our memories of my dad, and put an unnecessary burden on all of our family relationships."

He added: "I was shocked and stunned when I found out that Sherry Bray was a company director."

Defending Bray, Nicholas Cotter said: "She is not your standard criminal. She is a lady with an impeccable work history, who has raised her two daughters single-handedly. She has made a profound mistake by switching on a computer and taking an image of it. It is a mistake that will stay with her for a long time. She fully accepts the distress and upset she has caused to the families of Mr Sala and Mr Latcham. She has no computer skills – she simply pressed a button on a computer. Miss Bray should have known better, she had the responsibility to know better – but she opened Pandora's box," Mr Cotter said.

Representing Ashford, Thomas Horder said that this is the "biggest mistake he has ever made. Not only is he deeply sorry, but he really is devastated and ashamed by his actions. He is not responsible for this image getting on to the Internet. He did not stop for one minute to think of the potential impact of his actions on others. He was acting on his own unhealthy interest."

Horder also said that it is unlikely Ashford re-watched Sala's mortuary footage as many times as he is charged with. He described how Ashford's job required him to sit in front of a bank of three very large computer screens – each divided into smaller screens showing the feeds from every camera CSS operates.

He said: "I don't want Your Honour to think that on a number of occasions he is playing the same footage over and over. The footage is playing in the corner of the larger screen whilst he is responding to different alerts." Judge Peter Crabtree postponed sentencing to 'think carefully' about their punishment in what he called a 'highly unusual' case.

After due consideration, he jailed Bray for 14 months and Ashford for five months. The judge said the offences were "driven by morbid curiosity" and in Ashford's case, "forensic science". The judge said they had taken place within "a culture" at the company where staff watched post-mortem examinations even though they "had no justification to do so".

DI Gemma Vinton, from Wiltshire Police, said: "While both Bray and Ashford did plead guilty at the first crown court hearing, this case clearly shows that those in a position of responsibility need to ensure they act to the highest moral standards, as well as having a thorough understanding of the law. No sentence will undo the additional unnecessary distress and heartache caused to the Sala and Latcham families, who have remained at the forefront of our thoughts throughout the investigation. I hope that the families will now be able to focus on grieving for Emiliano and Andrew."

Anthony Johns, from the Crown Prosecution Service, said Bray and Ashford had caused "immense suffering" to grieving relatives. He added: "It is impossible to imagine why anyone would wish to record or view these sorts of images in such a flagrant breach of confidentiality and human decency."

13: DAVID HENDERSON

IN THE MONTHS FOLLOWING THE CRASH WILLIE McKay's usual pilot, David Henderson, proved elusive to the media and Cardiff City but the law eventually caught up with him when he was apprehended by police on suspicion of manslaughter by an unlawful act. A spokesperson for Dorset Police said a 64-year-old man from North Yorkshire had been arrested and released while investigations continue.

Detective Inspector Simon Huxter, of Dorset Police, said: "We have carried out a wide-ranging investigation into the circumstances of the death of Mr Sala and continue to work with partner agencies including the Civil Aviation Authority. As part of this investigation we have to consider whether there is any evidence of any suspected criminality and as a result of our inquiries we have today, Wednesday June 19 2019, arrested a 64-year-old man from the North Yorkshire area on suspicion of manslaughter by an unlawful act. He is assisting with our inquiries and has been released from custody under investigation."

Although not named by the police, it quickly became clear that Henderson was the man arrested. Family Liaison Officers kept the Sala and Ibbotson families updated with events.

The police statement continued: "This matter therefore is still subject to a live investigation and I would ask the media and members of the public to refrain from speculation, as this could cause additional distress to the families involved as well as potentially hinder the investigation. As is standard practice, we will not be releasing any further information as to the identity of the individual who has been arrested unless that person is charged to appear in court and again would discourage any speculation in relation to this."

Yet it was inevitable this police announcement would cause a media frenzy with Henderson released from custody but still under investigation. The media had been on Henderson's trail for some time, but stepped up their pursuit following his arrest, again to no avail. The *Daily Mail* reported how they had tried to contact Henderson at his home in York, but there was no response from the property and neighbours said he and his wife had headed out earlier in the evening for dinner.

Neighbours in the village of Hotham said the couple didn't seem to be worried. One said: "Their son has been up for a few days with his baby which is nearly a year old. The son, Tom, left with his wife and the baby earlier in the afternoon. Dave carried his suitcase to the car. Dave and Debbie then left separately." Another neighbour said, "They were dressed up for the evening. They often go out and don't get back until late. We have not noticed anything strange and he has not seemed worried about anything."

Sister-in-law Mandy Chandler refused to tell *Sun* reporters his whereabouts when there was no answer at Henderson's large stone house where he lives with his wife Debbie. Ms Chandler had "no idea" when they would be returning. Asked about the circumstances of her brother in law's arrest, she said: "I'm sorry I can't help you. I honestly do not know very much at all."

One resident said: "Dave and Debbie keep themselves to themselves. We knew he was a pilot. He was actually in the air when 9/11 happened, so we are told." Another neighbour said: "We haven't seen any police activity around the house."

The *Telegraph*'s Ben Rumsby was one of many making enquiries at the house after the autopsy report, but like everyone else he only got to talk to neighbours, one of whom told him "it was a media circus outside his home."

Henderson and his family acted quickly when the plane first went missing to stop further press enquiries, but as more facts emerged, it was more in the public interest for the media to continue their pursuit of Henderson, but they have so far failed to catch up with him.

When Henderson was initially feared dead after the flight plan for the doomed plane lodged with the French authorities named him as the pilot, the father-of-two was forced to post a Facebook message the next day stating that rumours of his death were untrue and his friend, David Ibbotson, had taken the controls instead and the media were naturally eager to contact his family for information. Henderson's daughter Kate contacted The Independent Press Standards Organisation (IPSO) having no doubt been advised to do so, because the family felt under siege, even more so when it was realised Henderson was still alive, and clearly had a story to tell. Kate wanted IPSO to inform the media to "stop contacting him and the rest of the family."

On January 24th, just three days after the tragic flight, Kate sent a request to IPSO's John Buckingham for the media to desist "any contact because Henderson was falsely named across various media outlets as the missing pilot in connection with the disappearance of a plane carrying footballer Emiliano Sala. Despite the error being identified he and I continue to receive calls and visits from members of the media. Neither he nor I shall be making any comment and request that journalists refrain form visiting our house."

Buckingham notified the media via a "private and confidential" email, that neither Henderson nor any members of his family wished to make any comment and Buckingham was happy to pass on this request, pointing out Clause 2 relating to privacy and Clause 3 referencing media harassment as part of the Editors Code of practise. It meant the media would be in breach of the regulations unless they could prove justification.

However, when it became clear that Henderson had played such a central role in the tragedy, the press felt he was fair game. Yet all calls, texts and visits by the media proved to be to no avail. Henderson made himself scarce. By now the Yorkshireman knew he was being targeted and not only by the media. He was under investigation by Dorset police.

More information about the flights emerged as The *Telegraph's* Ben Rumsby reported, there were concerns over whether other flights were properly licensed following the emergence of remarkable new details about the journeys Willie McKay and his agent son, Mark, had organised in the build-up to Sala's fatal flight.

The *Telegraph* disclosed that a plane previously piloted by the lead singer of Iron Maiden, Bruce Dickinson, "which was even once branded with his name and the band's insignia" had been used to fly Sala to and from Cardiff for contract talks. Another flight arranged by McKay while he was helping broker Sala's move to Cardiff had been piloted by Lord Porchester, the heir to the stately home from the television series Downton Abbey.

This and other information was provided to The *Telegraph* by aviation trade body the Air Charter Association (BACA), which obtained it as part of ongoing concerns about the flight that killed Sala. BACA claimed that the data covering about 10 trips arranged by McKay warranted a "full investigation" by the Civil Aviation Authority. That was "welcomed" by Cardiff, who also called for "industry-wide, enforceable safeguards to be put in place to ensure no further tragedies occur".

The BACA data shows that, like Sala's fatal flight, all the journeys arranged as part of the striker's transfer were non-commercial, and therefore subject to strict rules governing their funding.

The first of them, which Cardiff manager Neil Warnock took to watch Sala play on Dec 5, was booked through a company called FlexiFly. Bob Matthews, who took McKay's booking, confirmed the trip to and from Nantes had been organised on a perfectly-lawful leasing basis. The next flight organised on Jan 8, again as part of a scouting trip by Warnock to watch Sala, was booked through Guernsey-based Channel Jets. The private charter company was launched in 2016 by Aeris Aviation, the chairman of which is former Iron Maiden front-man Bruce Dickinson. According to the BACA data, the plane to and from Nantes was flown by Dickinson's chief executive, David Hayman.

The data also shows McKay used Channel Jets twice more, firstly for Sala's contract talks in which Dickinson's one-time Iron Maiden-branded plane was used, and then again for the player's medical.

The only other trip not arranged through Channel Jets was undertaken by Lord Porchester, who confirmed he had flown Sala's personal agent, Meïssa N'Diaye, back to Paris from Cardiff following the medical. The son of the Earl of Carnarvon and the heir to Highclere Castle, Lord Porchester owns a Piper light aircraft similar to that involved in Sala's fatal flight. He stated he had received no payment for the trip, something which would make it entirely lawful.

The Chief Executive of BACA, Dave Edwards, said his concerns over flights organised by McKay extended beyond their legality. He said: "Commercial flights operate under an entirely different framework to private ones. With a private flight, it is just one pilot there to protect the travelling public. There is no behind-the-scenes depth and breadth to the safety management. The travelling public need a fuller and better understanding of the additional risks they are putting themselves under when they choose any option other than a commercial charter flight."

Willie McKay had previously claimed he would have used Hayman again for Sala's final trip to say goodbye to his Nantes team-mates but the pilot was unavailable.

Asked about the licensing of Channel Jets' flights for McKay, Hayman referred The *Telegraph* to the CAA, saying "all data on them had been provided to the regulator". The CAA refused to comment on whether it would investigate the other McKay-organised flights or was already doing so. McKay also ignored requests for comment by The *Telegraph* on how they were funded, having previously confirmed in writing that at least two of them were "paid for" by his son, Mark.

Willie McKay admitted paying the full cost of the flight that Sala and pilot Dave Ibbotson were on when it crashed, rather than on the cost-sharing basis stipulated by regulations governing the trip. The Scot repeatedly stated the journey was booked via Henderson, an experienced light-aircraft pilot who had flown him around Europe on many occasions, and that he had no input into the selection of pilot or plane.

His failure to comment publicly on any of McKay's claims and his evasion of the media meant his role in the tragedy remains shrouded in mystery. Now, following his arrest, the evidence he has provided to police is something on which many cases may hinge.

The Flights

<u>5 December 2018</u> – Flight from Stapleford in Essex to Nantes – carrying Cardiff City manager Neil Warnock, assistant manager Kevin Blackwell, Willie McKay and Mark McKay to see Emiliano Sala play against Marseilles

<u>6 December</u> – party returns from Nantes to Cardiff.
Both flights made on G-KARE, operated by Surrey-based Flexifly Aircraft Hire Ltd

<u>8 January 2019</u> – Flight from Cardiff to Nantes – carrying Neil Warnock, Cardiff City Player Liaison Officer Callum Davies, Willie and Mark McKay to meet Sala and his agent. They're flown back to Cardiff the same day.
On N531EA, owned by Guernsey-based Channel Jets.

<u>14 January</u> – Sala's agent, Meïssa N'Diaye, flown from Paris to Nantes. N'Diaye and Sala are flown from Nantes to Cardiff to have a look around the Cardiff City Stadium, returning to Nantes the same day. Mr N'Diaye is then flown back to Paris.
All flights made on N843TE - owned by Channel Jets

<u>18 January</u> – Sala flies from Nantes to Cardiff for a medical and to sign his contract with Cardiff City. *Via Channel Jets in N531EA.* Sala's agent Mr N'Diaye - who has travelled to Cardiff for the signing via a commercial flight returned to Paris *by Lord George Porchester in his own aircraft, N14EF*

<u>19 January</u> – Sala flown back to Nantes by David Ibbotson on N264DB to bid farewell to his Nantes team-mates and make personal arrangements. Mr Ibbotson books into a hotel to await the return leg of the journey – on 21 January – to deliver Sala back to Cardiff for his first training session

<u>21 January</u> – The flight leaves Nantes at 19:15 and disappears from radar around an hour into the journey.

14: A TWIST IN THE TALE

IN AUGUST TOXICOLOGY TEST RESULTS ON Emiliano Sala's body showed carbon monoxide levels in his blood were so great it could have caused a seizure, unconsciousness or a heart attack. That chilling revelation led one of the characters deeply immersed in the investigations to remark, "Was it murder after all?"

For the family of David Ibbottson there was sufficient justification to suggest that after months of speculation surrounding the competence of the pilot, perhaps he hadn't been at fault after all and that perhaps the plane was at fault and had not been maintained to the proper standards. This latest development led to renewed demands for the wreckage to be salvaged to give up more clues from the deep. The Sala family demanded a detailed examination of the plane, while the body of the pilot had still yet to be found.

Daniel Machover of Hickman & Rose solicitors, who represent Sala's family, said "that dangerously high levels of carbon monoxide have been found in Emiliano's body raises many questions for the family. How he died will be determined at the inquest in due course. The family believe that a detailed technical examination of the plane is necessary. The family and the public need to know how the carbon monoxide was able to enter the cabin. Future air safety rests on knowing as much as possible on this issue. Emiliano's family call on the AAIB to salvage the wreckage of the plane without further delay."

Aided by their legal team, the Sala family insisted they would do everything possible to ensure the truth about the accident is revealed. The family added in a statement, issued through their solicitor, "Emiliano's family have been disappointed by the AAIB's response to Emiliano's death. They were especially surprised when, in the immediate aftermath of the incident, it appeared that the

AAIB had given up on conducting a full search for the aeroplane so it fell on them to do that. Without David Mearns locating the plane, Emiliano's body might never have been recovered and the potential significance of carbon monoxide poisoning of him and the pilot would never have been known.

"The family still hope that the inquest process will provide them with the answers they seek in relation to Emiliano's death and that air safety will be improved, including the prevention of similar deaths in future. They hope that their faith in English justice is not betrayed. The family are keeping all options on the table as to their next move. They will do everything possible to ensure that the truth about this terrible accident is revealed, so no family has to go through the same torment."

David Ibbotson's wife Nora agreed that recovering the plane could help find answers. She told Sky News it had "never occurred to her that carbon monoxide could potentially have played a part, as it was all about the weather and things like that. This has come out of the blue and it's a massive shock. I didn't realise that could have happened. Adding, "You can't smell it. You can't see it. It's lethal, they wouldn't have known. So it's nothing to do with the flying or anything like that, it's down to the aircraft."

Nora added that it should change how her husband is regarded by the general public. "It makes a big difference because they've been poisoned, they had no idea, it's a lethal gas. It's not going to change my situation, I've lost a husband, a father, a grandfather. Nothing can repay that, and change it. It's just one of the circumstances I've been caught up in. I've had to ignore [criticism]. I've got children to look after and I've got to go forward, I can't do any other. I've got to ignore what they're saying until the truth comes out. Maybe one way of finding out [what happened] is to bring the plane up if it can be done safely."

However the AAIB reiterated their view that recovering the aircraft would be costly and wouldn't add significantly to the investigation into the crash, "the reasons for our decision not to recover the aircraft wreckage have been explained in detail to both families concerned," a statement from the AAIB read. "In February our underwater search operation successfully located the wreckage, recovered the passenger's body and captured substantial video evidence from the scene using a remotely operated vehicle. It was not possible at the time to recover the wreckage. We have carefully considered the feasibility and merits of returning to attempt to recover the wreckage. In this case, we consider that it will not add significantly to the investigation and we will identify the correct safety issues through other means. In making our decision, we took into account the high cost of underwater recovery, the evidence we collected in February and the risk that, after a violent impact with the sea, the wreckage would not yield definitive evidence."

The statement said after a "violent impact with the sea", the wreckage may not even give definitive answers and the reasons for not retrieving the plane had been explained in detail to both the Sala and Ibbotson families.

The AAIB found Sala's blood had a COHb (carboxyhaemoglobin - which forms in red blood cells upon contact with carbon monoxide) level of 58%. At that level symptoms would include seizure, unconsciousness and heart attack. It added: "A COHb level of more than 50% in an otherwise healthy person is generally considered to be potentially fatal."

Piston engine aircraft such as the Piper Malibu involved in the crash produce high levels of carbon monoxide. The gas is normally conveyed away from the aircraft through the exhaust system, but poor sealing or leaks into the heating and ventilation system can enable it to enter the cabin. Several devices are available to alert pilots over the presence of carbon monoxide - they are not mandatory but can "alert pilots or passengers to a potentially deadly threat".

Retired pilot and aviation safety commentator Terry Tozer said the finding was "a surprise", adding: "It shows you can never tell what the root cause of an accident is until the investigators have dug into the nitty gritty. How and why did the carbon monoxide get in? Presumably through the exhaust system, the fumes get into the ventilation system." He said he had never encountered anything similar before and would not expect carbon monoxide poisoning to be a big risk on such an aircraft adding, "It's not like a car where you can open the windows. It can creep up on you, and that could be a slow process. It's odourless so you wouldn't necessarily know you were being fed these fumes unless you had a detection system – but that isn't mandatory for this type of aircraft."

Tozer agreed with the Sala family that salvaging the wreckage and examining it would be the only way to find how the leak occurred. "Aviation accidents usually come about when a number of factors accumulate. So, we start with the pilot and his lack of qualifications, then circumstances that delay the flight to night time, possibly feeling under pressure the pilot then takes off when he shouldn't and finds weather that he is struggling with and the final straw is that his ability is impaired by poisoning from a leak in the exhaust and he loses control."

AAIB investigators were working with aircraft manufacturers in the USA, where the Piper Malibu was registered, to look at how carbon monoxide could have entered the cabin. "Operational, technical and human factors" will be considered. Geraint Herbert, the AAIB's lead inspector for this investigation, said: "Symptoms at low exposure levels [to carbon monoxide] can be drowsiness and dizziness, but as the exposure level increases, it can lead to unconsciousness and death. The investigation continues to look into a wide range of areas in relation to this accident, but in particular we are looking at the potential ways in which carbon monoxide can enter the cabin in this type of aircraft."

Cardiff City were "concerned" by the report, adding, "we continue to believe that those who were instrumental in arranging its [the plane's] usage are held to account for this tragedy."

That statement provoked an angry response from Willie McKay, who clearly felt it pointed the finger at him yet again, and he let his feelings known with another rant at chairman Mehmet Dalman, the tone was, as usual, quite threatening, which was nevertheless surprising given that he had been advised by the Met Police to back off from any more threats. Cardiff let it be known that they would back any crowd-funding or financing needed to help salvage the plane to search for further clues. However, the club did not want the findings to detract from a potential culpability or negligence case.

Earlier the cause of Sala's death was officially given as "head and trunk injuries", according to the post-mortem examination, an opening inquest at Dorset Coroner's Court heard.

A pre-inquest review in November was told that the wreckage of the plane had 'washed away'. Earlier, a notice of the inquest gave the date and place of Sala's death as February 7 at Portland, and his place of residence as France.

The Sala family had organised for a further sonar survey of the crash site on October 22 which found that the wreckage was no longer there apart from possibly a number of smaller parts. David Ibbotson's widow Nora attended the pre-inquest review held in Bournemouth.

Matthew Reeve, representing the family, said that they took the decision to carry out the search after the Air Accidents Investigation Branch decided it was not necessary to revisit the crash scene or recover the wreckage. He said: "The family disagree with the decision not to salvage the wreckage. The aircraft wreckage is no longer present near to the location and some debris likely to be remains of the aircraft may not remain in place very long."

Coroner Rachael Griffin asked the AAIB why the aircraft was not being recovered considering toxicology results from a post mortem showed that Sala had carbon monoxide in his bloodstream.

Geraint Herbert, senior inspector for the AAIB, said the decision to not recover the wreckage had been taken as it felt it had identified safety issues without the need to further examine the crashed plane. He said that the safety of divers and the practicality of recovering the wreckage had to be taken into consideration.

He added that it would not be possible to determine whether damage seen on the crashed plane would have occurred prior to the crash, during the impact or while under the water. Mr Herbert said: "We decided we wouldn't be going back and nothing I have heard subsequently has changed my mind."

Detective Inspector Simon Huxter, of Dorset Police, said inquiries continued following the arrest earlier of a 64-year-old man from North Yorkshire on suspicion of manslaughter by an unlawful act. He said: "Our investigations continue. It's not reached a conclusion and therefore we are still continuing inquiries to establish whether there is any evidence of criminality."

At the request of Sala's family, the coroner called on the police to preserve any blood samples to ensure they can be made subject to further independent testing if needed. And she said she would write to the pathologist, Dr Basil Purdue, to ask what led to further testing earlier this year for carbon monoxide.

Mrs Griffin adjourned the proceedings for a further pre-inquest review on March 16 to enable the Civil Aviation Authority and the AAIB to conclude their investigations but warned the inquest could be suspended if a criminal prosecution was launched.

Mrs Griffin said: "Can I offer my condolences to Mr Sala's family? I also want to offer my sympathies to Mrs Ibbotson and Mr Ibbotson's family after the incident and due to the fact Mr Ibbotson remains missing until this date."

A source told me that Cardiff sent a legal representative to the hearing, and had paid for the new sonar search for the wreckage, which they thought wouldn't have cost over £20,000.

15: THE LEGAL BATTLE

FROM AS EARLY AS THE WEEK OF THE CRASH, a series of legal cases seemed inevitable involving both football clubs, the families of the deceased and the agent(s) of Emiliano Sala. Since then cases have come before FIFA, the governing body of football, several magistrates and will inevitably end up at CAS, the Court of Arbitration for Sport. The prospects for it all ending up in the High Court in London are growing with each revelation. Even as this book was being finalised events surrounding this incredible case seemed to take a different turn almost every week with allegations and possible prosecutions for a variety of offences that even a hardened journalist like myself could not have anticipated. With that in mind it is appropriate at this point to introduce the various legal eagles and PR gurus who represent the parties.

In Cardiff City's corner is Chris Nott of Capital Law and George Tucker, Senior Vice President in Mercury's London PR office. Nott was at the heart of all the legal aspects in the Sala saga, and there are many! The founder of Capital Law and a director of the firm's integrated HR management consultancy, Capital People, he founded Capital Law in 2006. A commercial lawyer for over 30 years, working mainly on business disputes, such as a £100m claim by employees against their former CEO who had misappropriated their shares, he represented owner Vincent Tan when he bought Cardiff City from previous owner and now Life President, Sam Hammam.

In 2016, Nott developed Capital Dispute Finance, a £50m fund to enable Capital's clients to finance litigation. For this, Capital was highly commended by The *Financial Times* Innovation Awards, *The Lawyer*, and *The Legal Week*, and won the Cardiff Business Award. He was Chair of the Welsh Government's F&PS

sector panel and is a member of its predecessor: the Ministerial Advisory Board. In 2016, he received an OBE for services to Business and Economic Development in Wales. He is the Prince of Wales' Business Ambassador for Wales. He's also a Director of the Cardiff Blues, and a founder of 'Knife and Fork Food'.

Willie McKay contacted Chris Nott in the aftermath of the crash and left a voice mail message that has been retained by the club's lawyers as they related to McKay trying to trace someone connected with the Welsh club, believing that this individual was briefing the media against him. As we have seen the threats led to a police investigation when McKay traced his victim to a London café.

Chris Nott was at the hub of legal issues such as issuing McKay with a letter warning him that action would be taken if he continued with his threats. He also liaised with local police through their regular point of contact, Sgt Wayne Palmer. The threats were taken seriously by those at the receiving end: one considered moving house, another hired several body guards while McKay's behaviour was also described as "a nuisance and distraction" from the main legal issues that Nott had to deal with.

The FIFA case has consumed a lot of his time, with an appeal an inevitability, as it might end up in the High Court. Claims of negligence were high on Cardiff's agenda. The possibility of defamation against McKay was raised but quickly dismissed as that would turn into a side-show and it was not necessarily relevant to much more important on-going issues.

Nott told me that he had nine lawyers working on an assortment of Cardiff City related cases, ranging from the four witness statements provided to the local police regarding McKay's death threat allegations, to the Sala personal contract, insurance, FIFA's adjudication on the transfer fee, potential legal action against Nantes and McKay for liability and gross negligence and handling litigation around the Sala family and their lawyers.

At least once a week, around midday, there is a conference call involving an update briefing from Nott to chairman Mehmet Dalman, CEO Ken Choo, and PR guru George Tucker.

The Legal Battle

Over the course of more than 17 years in corporate affairs and communications, Tucker has worked in-house within government and for consultancies advising multi-national businesses across the world on their corporate engagement strategies. Prior to joining Mercury, George was the Head of Communications for Imperial Tobacco in the UK having spent six years with the UK Foreign & Commonwealth office, latterly as a diplomat in Kenya responsible for managing the UK's engagement at the highest level with Kenyan counterparts. He was also engaged on South Asian politics and handled the UK's engagement on a broad range of economic, political and security issues with Pakistan, India and Bangladesh.

George also spent five years focused on the Middle East as a Corporate and Financial Communications consultant, primarily advising businesses from London on their investor relations and corporate engagement strategies into the UAE, Qatar, Bahrain and Kuwait. He then moved to the Middle East and ran regional offices for both Gavin Anderson and then Brunswick out of Abu Dhabi where he advised some of the region's biggest institutions and government departments on their international external engagement strategies. George began his career with Bell Pottinger Public Affairs, focusing on finance, automotive and manufacturing clients. He holds a BA in German and European Politics from Bristol University, and has lived and worked throughout Europe, including time in-house with BMW and EADS. He and his wife, Trish, have two girls and live near Cirencester.

Nantes team of lawyers are led by Jérôme Marsaudon and Louis Marie Absil of Reinhart Marville Torre based in Paris. Jérôme is engaged primarily in judicial and arbitration business law litigation. He advises his clients on complex company law litigation, disputes between shareholders and liability guarantee issues. He benefits from an active and continuous practice in contractual matters, enabling him to assist the firm's clients in drafting, implementing and terminating their contracts, particularly in commercial matters. He is involved in sports law litigation for professional sport clubs. In 2003, he joined the firm's litigation department where he was made partner in January 2010.

Louis-Marie Absil is ranked among the best commercial litigation and criminal business law lawyers by Legal 500 and Chambers. He regularly represents the firm's clients before civil, commercial and criminal courts and in the context of ad hoc arbitration proceedings. He is primarily involved in company law and shareholder disputes and in commercial litigation related, in particular, to non-performance and premature termination of contracts. He also advises the firm's clients in financial and economic criminal law. He is renowned for his mastery of preventive measures and crisis situations.

Nantes Public Relations are handled by Guillaume Didier. He has served as examining magistrate in the office of the fight against terrorism and vice-prosecutor, in charge of relations with the press, to the public prosecutor of the Republic of Paris, Jean-Claude Marin. He is press and communication advisor to the cabinets of the Ministers of Justice and the Minister of Foreign Affairs. Since 2011 Guillaume had been in charge of a mission to improve judicial communication at the Ministry of Justice.

Nantes team were quickly on the offensive, in line with the French club's swift demand for payment of the first tranche of Sala's transfer fee before the player's body had even been recovered from the sea. Below is an email conversation between myself and Guillame concerning Sala's contract. I started by asking for a response to Cardiff's claims that the contract was not valid.

GUILLAME: "The transfer contract is valid, it has been registered by FIFA. FC Nantes has completed all the required paperwork to complete the Emiliano Sala transfer. Thus, FIFA registered the International Transfer Certificate (CIT) on 21 January 2019 at 5H30 PM. Nantes is fully compliant with FIFA rules. As for Emiliano Sala's registration in the Premier League, FC Nantes has no information about it. And if it could be a problem for Cardiff, it is not a problem for Nantes. However, it does not concern FIFA's validation of the transfer, which was confirmed on 21 January with the dispatch of the International Transfer Certificate (CIT) to FC Nantes.

As for the contractual relations between Nantes and McKay, this has no connection with the subject and is subject to conventional confidentiality agreements.

HH: Thanks for all this, Guillaume. We have been told that the transfer agreement between Cardiff and Nantes contained several preconditions which, unless met, would render that agreement null and void. We're told that one of them was that Sala was registered to play in the Premier League and another was that his employment contract was valid. As the Premier League rejected his employment contract, neither of those preconditions would have been met. We're told Sala's employment contract would have had to have been renegotiated before it could be resubmitted to the Premier League. Does Nantes dispute that such an agreement with Cardiff existed, one that without these two things taking place rendered that agreement null and void?

GUILLAME: Nantes confirmed that all the paperwork was completed for the transfer with the French League.

HH: Thank you very much. This is perfect. However, the first part is about the paperwork with the French League. Is it correct that Nantes have agreed that all the paperwork was not completed for the transfer with the French League?

GUILLAME: FC Nantes has completed all the required paperwork to complete the Emiliano Sala transfer. Thus, FIFA registered the International Transfer Certificate (CIT) on 21 January 2019 at 5H30 PM.
Nantes is fully compliant with FIFA rules.
As for Emiliano Sala's registration in the Premier League, FC Nantes has no information about it. And if it could be a problem for Cardiff, it is not a problem for Nantes.
However, it does not concern FIFA's validation of the transfer, which was confirmed on 21st January with the dispatch of the International Transfer Certificate (CIT) to FC Nantes.
About FC Nantes' request: as Cardiff City has still not paid the

first part of Emiliano Sala's transfer, FC Nantes has made a request to FIFA, on 26th February 2019. By letter of 15th March, FIFA confirmed that it had registered the request filed by FC Nantes and said it gave Cardiff club until April 3 to respond.

The Sala Family are also well represented with prominent QC Michael Mansfield representing them, as the *Telegraph* reported. Michael Mansfield also represented most of the victims' families at the recent Hillsborough inquests.

Prominent QC Michael Mansfield agrees to represent family of Emiliano Sala

25 MARCH 2019

The family of Emiliano Sala has instructed one of the UK's most prominent QCs in a bid to ensure anyone responsible for his tragic death is made to "pay".

Michael Mansfield, who represented most of the victims' families at the recent Hillsborough Inquests, has agreed to help Sala's relatives secure what his mother last week described as "justice for Emiliano".

Mansfield's Nexus Chambers yesterday confirmed he had been instructed by the family of the striker, who was killed in a plane crash over the English Channel two days after Cardiff City announced his signing from Nantes.

Nexus declined to comment further on what it said was an "ongoing case" amid speculation Sala's family could pursue a negligence claim over his January 21 death.

Mansfield's chambers profile describes the QC as having tackled "some of the most controversial legal cases this country has seen".

As well as representing the families in the 2014-16 inquests into the death of 96 people at the Hillsborough Disaster, he has represented Mohammed Al Fayed in his pursuit of the truth surrounding the death of his son, Dodi, and Princess Diana, the families of victims at the Bloody Sunday Inquiry, the Birmingham Six, the family of the murdered teenager Stephen Lawrence, and the family of Jean Charles de Menezes, shot by the Metropolitan Police in 2005.

He is currently representing survivors and relatives of victims at the Grenfell Tower Inquiry and survivors at the Independent Inquiry into Child Sex Abuse.

Confirmation of his instruction by Sala's family comes less than a week after the player's mother angrily accused Cardiff City of showing "disrespect towards my family" by withholding the striker's £15 million transfer fee from Nantes. Mercedes Taffarel also told *L'Equipe* she had heard nothing since his death from Willie McKay, who booked the flight on which Sala was killed.

She added: "All I'm saying is that I want justice for my son. I simply want the truth. Let justice determine if there has been negligence, if someone made a mistake, and make them pay."

Cardiff and Nantes declined to comment on Mansfield's appointment, while McKay did not respond to requests for comment.

Sources have told the *Daily Telegraph* the Welsh club are committed to ensuring Sala's family are looked after, despite their withholding of his transfer fee from Nantes over an agreement they claim became "null and void" when he died.

McKay, who helped broker Sala's move to Cardiff, previously said he was willing to meet the player's mother.

Daniel Machover is a leading solicitor in civil liberties, police law, prison law and public and administrative law, who is in constant touch with the Sala family. He is "pioneering and dedicated", "a guru in inquests" and "someone whose work changes the law for the better," according to the 2016 edition of Chambers. Previous editions describe him as "a giant in the field" of civil liberties, "an expert in public and administrative law and an expert in fighting cases against police forces: with his knowledge and experience he is one of the best around", and an "extremely bright, sharp and experienced lawyer" who is "very astute, very intelligent and very passionate", with "a first-class ability to think creatively and assimilate the facts of a case swiftly and thoroughly, with a tactical approach"; and a "...fantastically sensible and committed lawyer who is not afraid to get stuck in and take on large challenges."

He specialises in civil litigation on behalf of people who have suffered wrongs at the hands of the criminal justice system. He has brought many successful claims against the Ministry of Justice, Home Office and police and has represented a wide range of individuals and companies at inquests. He acts for individuals and businesses in civil claims which have a criminal element, such as his successful defence in 2016 of politician's son Max Bakiev, who fought off allegations made in the High Court in London of a brutal, commercially-motivated attack on a representative of a gold exploration company in Kyrgyzstan. His test cases include the right of prisoners to vote, the frequency of review of lifers' release dates and the application of the Human Rights Act to officials acting outside the United Kingdom. He brought the successful and ground-breaking group action for prisoners alleging assault and systemic management failures in HMP Wormwood Scrubs during the 1990s.

In recognition of his work, he received the Margery Fry Award from the Howard League for Penal Reform for "ensuring the protection of prisoners through the tenacious pursuit of legal remedies". He has a worldwide reputation in the field of international human rights law. His work for victims of war crimes, torture and crimes against humanity has placed him at the forefront of the movement for universal criminal jurisdiction. His cases have included some of the most serious human rights violations and he has helped to establish the equal application of the rule of law in all circumstances. In light of his expertise, he has been invited to address members of the European and UK Parliaments in London and Brussels on the theme of universal jurisdiction.

He joined Hickman & Rose in 1997 as head of the Civil Litigation department and became a partner in 1998. He is currently Chair of INQUEST, the charity which provides a specialist, comprehensive advice service to bereaved people on contentious deaths and their investigation.

The PR army was complete with Dan Newling, Head of Communications for solicitors Hickman & Rose who were representing the family's interests. He oversees all aspects of Hickman & Rose's external communications. His responsibilities include: developing the communications strategies which will achieve the firm's long-term business ambitions, creating bespoke PR campaigns designed to win positive coverage in the national and specialist media, overseeing reactive and crisis media relations on behalf of the firm, and occasionally its client and generating, writing and editing expert opinion and analysis articles on behalf of the firm's partners. In addition he describes one of his main skills as "Hijacking breaking news with relevant expert quotes to win positive press coverage and overseeing the firm's branding, social media output and website."

He describes himself as "formerly an award-winning newspaper journalist and documentary film maker, and non-fiction book author". His web site boasts of making "a standalone special documentary about the Grenfell Tower disaster for BBC 2 and an hour long investigation into FIFA for the BBC's Panorama." He was part of the BBC Panorama team which won the Foreign Press Association;s award for an investigation into corruption at football's governing body. In addition: "I've made numerous short films for BBC Newsnight and developed documentary programmes and series for international broadcasters including HBO and ITV. I've also written a book about a murder and miscarriage of justice in South Africa."

The first legal case directly concerning the clubs was adjudicated on by FIFA whose president, Gianni Infantino, had described the death of Emiliano Sala as a tragedy, and hoped the two clubs could come to an agreement. However following when it became clear that the clubs were at loggerheads over the transfer fee payments FIFA bodies were in place to adjudicate.

A spokesman for Cardiff said prior to the decision, "Cardiff City remains committed to ensuring fairness and accountability with respect to the agreement between Cardiff City and FC Nantes, but first and foremost the relevant authorities must be allowed to determine the facts surrounding this tragedy. It is inappropriate to comment further at this stage."

In the days after the crash Mehmet Dalman confirmed the French club had threatened legal action, but Cardiff were seeking "clarification" on the status of Sala. "Of course, if we are contractually obliged to pay them then of course we will. We are an honourable club. But if we are not – and there are some anomalies in that – then surely you would expect me as the chairman and guardian of this club's interests to look into that and hold our position. That is what we are doing. We are still in the process of gathering information and that process will be ongoing. And when we reach a level where we have enough information, I am sure we will sit down with Nantes and move forward."

Cardiff were looking to get a full picture of events. "[Nantes] have asked for what they believe is the money due to them" Dalman continued, "and there is a process and they have initiated that process. What we are saying is, that we are not in agreement with that process given the extraordinary events that have taken place and the tragic circumstances. We are not making any positive or negative statements. We are simply saying, please understand there are a lot of questions which need to be answered and that is what we are trying to do."

Nantes wrote to Cardiff on 5 February, just 15 days after the crash and before Sala's body had been recovered, requesting the first instalment of the transfer fee. Cardiff said they were withholding payment until investigations were complete and they were satisfied about "anomalies" around the deal. Dalman pledged Cardiff would be "honourable" if they are contractually obliged to pay. Sala's ill-fated transfer has not been included by the Football Association in its annual list of transactions involving agents.

Under FIFA rules, the FA has published the total payments made by clubs in England's top five divisions to football agents for the last three years. It also publishes every transaction - loan, transfer or renegotiated deal - that involved an agent, listing who represented the player and the clubs. That list runs to 17 tightly-typed spreadsheets, with around 600 transactions for Premier League clubs alone, including 23 for Cardiff. One of Cardiff's 'intermediary transactions' involved manager Neil Warnock's son James, who works for Unique Sports Management and represents Bluebirds forward Rhys Healey. The Sala transfer was not included in the list because it is under dispute and being reviewed by FIFA.

Sala's previous club Bordeaux were claiming a 50 per cent sell on fee. Sala spent three years at the club before moving to Nantes, although Bordeaux released a statement on their club website saying they were owed no money from the deal and denying they made any claims. The statement in French, translates as: "Bordeaux formally denies the information published that the club claimed its 'due' from the transfer of Emiliano Sala. In these sad circumstances, Bordeaux express their support for Sala's family and friends."

Yet a FIFA ruling on September 30th instructed Cardiff City to pay the first £5.3m instalment of Sala's transfer to Nantes. From Cardiff's perspective they found it incredible that the football's governing body had announced the decision without hearing from both sides, so it instantly caused a storm of controversy, and the reaction from the club was inevitable and they took their appeal to the Court of Arbitration for Sport (CAS).

FIFA's briefing to the media was that the executive, led by the President, would have liked to have seen some sort of compromise split over the fee, but the independent commission found that the complaint that the first instalment had not been paid was upheld, and that subsequent complaints, if the next two instalments were withheld, as expected, would also be upheld. The second instalment was due in January 2020. Cardiff chairman Mehmet Dalman and the Board immediately sought clarification from FIFA that those indeed were the findings, but the club suspected that the FIFA committee had upheld the contract totally in Nantes favour and they would launch an immediate appeal to CAS and to the High Court if necessary.

Had FIFA opted for a compromise of a split fee, or had it been no more than the first instalment, then Cardiff would have reached out to Nantes to discuss a further compromise and worked toward accepting the decision. However a source inside the club told me that if, "FIFA want to go to war, we shall go to war".

The controversial decision was taken by a committee led by South African Football Association chief executive Raymond Hack nine months after the player died in a plane crash. Hack, in his capacity as chairman of the players' status committee of FIFA, dissected the arguments at FIFA's Zurich headquarters. Reports that the committee had personally heard from the legal representatives of both clubs was denied by Cardiff. Hack's deputy, Mahfuza Akhter from Bangladesh, is one of the most high-powered women in football. Hack also serves as the chairman of disciplinary committee of the Confederation of African Football (CAF) and made the decision that awarded the African Champions League title to Tunisia's Esperance after the walk off in the final by opponents Wydad Casablanca. The 69-year-old Johannesburg lawyer is also an arbitrator for the World Anti-Doping Agency (WADA) and sits on the ethics committee of FINA, world swimming's controlling body.

Cardiff continued their argument that they cannot be held liable for the fee because Sala was not officially their player, despite the Argentinian visiting the club and signing a contract. Cardiff produced evidence that the transfer was null and void because the Premier League rejected clauses that were requested by Nantes in the original contract and that Sala never had a chance to review or sign the final version which still had to be amended, so he was not registered as a Premier League player. Nantes' counter claim was that the required paperwork was completed as far as they were concerned and registered with FIFA and the FA of Wales.

Hack gave the clubs opportunities to reach a settlement in the dispute but they failed to even come together for mediation, despite Cardiff offering a meeting. As Sala's move was an international transfer, it had to go through FIFA's mandatory system. The International Transfer Certificate was completed but there were issues with the separate matter of Premier League registration. The ITC was registered with the Football Association of Wales and confirmed Sala as a Cardiff player. Cardiff had ten days to appeal to CAS in Lausanne following the FIFA decision.

"Cardiff City FC acknowledges the decision announced today by FIFA's Players' Status Committee regarding the transfer of Emiliano Sala. We will be seeking further clarification from FIFA on the exact meaning of their statement in order to make an informed decision on our next steps," read a club statement.

A statement issued by FC Nantes' lawyers, Jérôme Marsaudon and Louis-Marie Absil, read: "We welcome this decision by FIFA. Cardiff must respect its commitments and the rules of sports law. Beyond the human tragedy that affected the entire sports community with the death of Emiliano Sala, FIFA has just reminded that the legal security of the commitments made by clubs in the context of player transfers must be respected.

"It is not a surprise, it confirms the position that FC Nantes has held for the last nine months: Emiliano Sala signed with Cardiff; his contract with Nantes was over; the international transfer contract (ITC), delivered by FIFA, states that on the day of the accident Emiliano was indeed a Cardiff player."

Like everything significant in the Sala case, it made news around the world, as did Cardiff's announcements they were heading for an appeal. The Welsh club confirmed it was "extremely disappointed" with the verdict of the governing body's Players' Status Committee. Cardiff said in a statement: "Following FIFA's update on their announcement regarding the transfer of Emiliano

Sala, Cardiff City Football Club will be launching an appeal to the Court of Arbitration for Sport. Cardiff City FC is extremely disappointed at the decision of the Players' Status Committee to award against the club. It would appear the committee has reached its conclusion on a narrow aspect of the overall dispute, without considering the full documentation presented by Cardiff City FC to FIFA.

"Nevertheless, there remains clear evidence that the transfer agreement was never completed in accordance with multiple contractual requirements which were requested by Nantes, thereby rendering it null and void."

Those requirements, according to Cardiff City sources, included a stipulation that the Football Association of Wales and France's Ligue de Football Professional had to confirm to both clubs that Sala "has been registered as a Cardiff City FC player and that the player's International Transfer Certificate has been released."

The Cardiff City statement continued: "We shall be appealing to CAS in order to seek a decision which considers all of the relevant contractual information and provides clarity on the full legal situation between our two clubs. This is a complex matter, which includes ongoing civil and criminal considerations both in the UK and abroad, which will likely have an impact on the validity of the transfer. It is therefore vital that a comprehensive judgement is reached following a full assessment and review of the facts."

Lawyers for Nantes had been silent since the beginning of the FIFA investigation. Jérôme Marsaudon and Louis-Marie Absil, of the firm RMT, explained their position to French newspaper *Ouest-France* and considered that "there could be no other way out".

Do you welcome the judgment of FIFA?

Jérôme Marsaudon: "It is only justice and there could be no other issues. Through this judgment, it affirms the validity of the transfer of Emiliano Sala to Cardiff and orders the application of the contract between the two clubs. This is a logical decision in light of the very objective elements that we had and we provided to FIFA. It was known that the player had terminated his contract with FC Nantes, that he had a new contract with Cardiff, that a CIT (International Transfer Certificate) had been issued and exchanged between the Federations shortly before the accident."

Louis-Marie Absil: "It's a human drama that Cardiff has tried to exploit to escape their obligations. FIFA reminds us that the legal certainty taken by contracts between clubs in a transfer must be respected. A questioning of the CIT would have weakened the whole system. Through this decision, it protects it and renews the validity of a framework."

After seven months of proceedings, it's a victory for FC Nantes?

Louis-Marie Absil: "In view of the dramatic circumstances, the emotion aroused, we should never have reached this point, nor try to create confusion through statements in the press mixing everything. Today, for us, there is still no room for bragging."

Jérôme Marsaudon: "That's why, from the beginning, we chose the strategy of silence in relation to the constant agitation of our opponents. We did not want to waste time and we had nothing to gain by getting into controversy. We only held a legal argument because we were always convinced that we were providing enough elements to FIFA judges to make a decision with confidence."

FIFA had advocated a conciliation between the two clubs. There was no risk in refusing it?

Jérôme Marsaudon: "I would like to remind you that it was FC Nantes who first reached out to Cardiff in the days following the tragedy. As the only answer he received an invitation to contact the lawyers of the Welsh club, and no longer had contacts thereafter."

Louis-Marie Absil: "We thought a lot about FIFA's invitation. With regard to the last seven months and Cardiff's behaviour, we have come to the conclusion that they have never been in any desire to reach an agreement. Their only purpose was to delay the process and save time to escape payment."

If Cardiff had to appeal to the Court of Arbitration for Sport, what interpretation should we make of it?

Louis-Marie Absil: "The supervisor has confirmed the validity of the contract, and this is essential. If Cardiff were to go to CAS, it would only confirm what they have been looking for from the beginning, namely to escape their obligations by all means."

The second payment of 6 million Euros is scheduled for January 2020. The third instalment of 5 million Euros is due in January 2021. Half of the total amount is due to the Girondins de Bordeaux, former club of Emiliano Sala.

Cardiff were incensed by Nantes' response, which included an interview by lawyers acting for the French club in which they accused Cardiff of exploiting the "human drama" of Sala's death to "escape their obligations". They also told *Ouest France* that the Welsh side had made no effort to strike a compromise agreement over their dispute beyond an invitation to contact their legal counterparts there. A source close to the club told the *Telegraph*: "Any suggestion the process was completed shows blatant disregard for the life of Emiliano Sala, who tragically died before he was able to review and sign a contract which would have been acceptable to the Premier League, meaning the process could not have been completed. It is alarming that Nantes seem focused entirely on retrieving money rather than honouring the memory of their player or engaging to determine how the clubs can support his family in any way. It is completely untrue that no effort was made to achieve conciliation with Nantes. They were invited to without-prejudice discussions on multiple occasions, via official channels, which they systematically and continuously rejected."

The source also revealed Cardiff's determination to avoid McKay and his son Mark getting their hands on the 10 per cent commission. "The intermediaries involved in this process at the instruction of Nantes should not be allowed to benefit financially following the tragic outcome."

The Cardiff City chairman Mehmet Dalman is leading a crusade for the rights of the Sala family and the financial health of his Championship club as he gave the inside track on why the fight goes on all the way to the High Court if necessary. Dalman told me: "The Sala family seem to be once again disregarded here. FIFA talk about payments to Nantes. What about payments to the Sala family? If anyone should be considered here financially compensated it is the family. It can't be right that all the money goes to Nantes and to the multitude of agents involved, with no consideration to the Sala family."

The Cardiff chairman stressed that this has never been a case for FIFA to handle and might not be within the remit of CAS, if they cannot deal with the wider aspects of this unique and disturbing case – in particular the legal and criminal aspects. Dalman explained: "There still remain so many questions unanswered. Just one for example is that if the player was an asset of Cardiff City, then what right did anyone have to make decisions on our behalf on vital issues about the pilot, the state of the plane and all aspects about the licensing to fly commercially. We still await the final verdict from the aviation authorities.

"In addition to the legal issues of negligence and liability, there is the criminal investigation by the police. It was only a few weeks ago that the police arrested someone on suspicion of manslaughter, and we have no idea where that investigation has led them to, and what conclusions they are likely to draw."

It is quite clear listening to Dalman deliberating on the FIFA decision to simply award Nantes judgement in their favour that he and his club are very angry. The financial implications will not be easy to absorb. He explains: "A club of our size do not have vast financial resources. Far from it. Our accounts are public knowledge, and it is quite obvious that we cannot afford to hand over a cheque for £15m without an asset of that value without heading toward bankruptcy. Yes, bankruptcy, it would be enough to send a club of our size in that direction. Paying out £15m without the asset of that value would not look very pretty on the balance sheet and if it wasn't for the club's owner Vincent Tan being prepared to put his hand in his pocket a club like ours could easily go under as it does not have that kind of resource."

Taking so much into account it is easy to see why FIFA's decision is hard for Cardiff to stomach, and they feel that their case has been handled without due consideration to *all* the facts. Dalman said: "We just didn't expect FIFA to be so poor in the way they have handled this. Yes, of course we fully respect FIFA as an organisation and respect their processes, and while everyone expected us to appeal, no one expected FIFA to look at this so narrowly. They have simply said, does a contact exist? And concluded that it does. Yet, we have all the evidence to suggest that it doesn't, while so much has yet to be forthcoming in terms of the legal and criminal aspects of this case which involved, in part, that contract issue."

Cardiff will go through the due processes and appeal to CAS but it is equally clear that ultimately the case is likely to end up in a court of law.

In documents relating to the grounds for the FIFA Players' Status Committee decision it was revealed that Cardiff faced a three-window transfer ban unless they paid the first instalment of the transfer fee to Nantes. Cardiff had been given 45 days from receiving Nantes bank details to hand over the first £5.3m payment, however as this countdown would be halted by a Cardiff appeal to CAS over the original decision, which is almost certain, then it was highly unlikely to be put into effect given Cardiff's previous pledge to honour the transfer if ruled to do so by the world's governing body.

A *Daily Mirror* report also claimed that Cardiff's refusal to pay Sala's transfer fee was causing problems for his boyhood club, San Martin de Progresso. The fifth-tier Argentinian club were owed

£110,000 from the transfer, funds they had planned to use to refurbish their ground, which had just been renamed in honour of the late striker on the day of his 29th birthday.

Sala played for the club for 10 years from the age of 5.

In late October a report claimed that Cardiff were in consultation with Eric Dupond-Moretti about lodging criminal proceedings against Nantes in the French courts. One source close to the case told me that it "will be like throwing a grenade into the mix" when told of the development.

The 58-year-old French criminal defence lawyer is famous for a record number of acquittals in French territories. Nicknamed "Acquittator" (an admix of acquitter and matador) in the courtrooms, he has a formidable reputation. According to his wikipedia page he has starred in 4 feature films and played himself in the Claire Denis film 'Bastards'. In 2013 he refused the Legion of Honour, the highest honour that can be bestowed on a French citizen.

This new line of potential litigation is clearly aimed in reverting to French law to examine whether criminal negligence has taken place. It is clear from Cardiff's submissions to FIFA that they hold Nantes responsible, as Willie McKay, who organised the plane journey, was effectively representing the French club. The reason for taking their case to the French courts is the greater likelihood of success in litigating this issue there.

The French law firm Dupond-Morertti & Vey boasts on its website: "Over the years, the firm has established itself as a benchmark, particularly in criminal defence, the promotion of fundamental rights and conducting complex litigation. Our structure is independent which means we can select a restricted number of cases so as to provide our clients with tailor-made support. When the technical nature of litigation requires it, we set up teams of professionals and collaborate with the best lawyers and experts in each discipline. We work throughout France and have acquired significant experience in courts abroad.

"The firm has developed expertise in the world of sport. We provide legal advice to French and foreign professional clubs, sports federations and top-level professional players in their contractual relations (drafting and performance of sports contracts, sponsoring, etc.). We assist them in their relations with agents and in management of their image rights (image rights contracts, actions in law by the press, etc.). Several of the firm's lawyers, experts in this field, also work as sports representatives

"Our recent work: Legal advice to a Top 14 professional rugby club in connection with application of a salary cap rule and defence before the regulatory bodies of the French Rugby Federation and the National Rugby League. Legal advice to a European football club in connection with a preliminary inquiry opened at the National Public Prosecutor's Office for Financial Affairs for suspicions of match-fixing in the Champions League. Defence of a top professional boxer, twice French champion, accused of acts of violence against a professional hockey player.

"Work on behalf of a football player with a major European club charged with offences of blackmail and attempted extortion in the context of an ongoing investigation. Defence of two professional handball players prosecuted before the Criminal Court for offences of complicity in fraud in connection with rigged matches. Defence of two stable managers before the High Commission of the Société d'Encouragement à l'Elevage du Cheval Français [SECF, French Association for Horse-Breeding] for offences of administration of banned substances."

Should Dupond-Moretti conclude that there is a good chance of success in the French courts, and Cardiff opt to go down the route of litigation, then the appeal to CAS of the FIFA decision to pay the transfer fee, would need to be postponed.

16: THIS WAS NO ACCIDENT

I T IS CLEAR FROM ALL THE EVIDENCE ACCRUED following the crash that this tragedy was not an unfortunate accident but a series of preventable errors with a tragic ending. Yet, as the anniversary of the incident draws near, the truth is no closer to being revealed. The Sala family have sought closure but now that their wish for the abandoned Piper PA-46 Malibu plane to be raised from the bottom of the English Channel has disappeared, what will the separate investigations by police, coroners and AAIB reveal that isn't already in the public domain? And how will the legal wrangles between both football clubs and Willie McKay or the potential prosecution of David Henderson be resolved? The likelihood remains that investigations will throw up more evidence and lead to other figures being dragged into a saga that threatens to run for years.

The overriding fear is that some of the most vital evidence in this case may have been lost when the wreckage of the plane was left to wash away. The toxicology report stating that Emiliano Sala's blood was contaminated with potentially deadly levels of carbon monoxide was a twist no one saw coming, least of all aviation experts who speculated on weather conditions and pilot error for the crash. It is almost certain that pilot David Ibbotson was affected by the odourless gas and initial assumptions may have been incorrect. Toxicology experts stated that anything above a 50% level is likely to cause "seizure, unconsciousness and heart attack". Sala's body showed he had a carbon monoxide saturation at 58 per cent. Given that he was considerably younger than Ibbotson, the chances are the pilot would have been affected even more strongly, which might explain the erratic flight pattern immediately before the crash.

Yet if it hadn't been for a privately-funded salvage operation,

Sala's body would not have been raised from the deep as authorities had already abandoned the scene citing the degree of difficulty due to inclement weather and costs involved. It seems odd given the significance of the findings that the same excuses were used to not pursue a salvage mission to recover the plane which has subsequently broken up on the sea bed – the absence of certainty the salvaged plane would be bring may already cast doubt on the AAIB's findings.

Given that the US-registered Piper Malibu N264DB was not licensed for commercial flying, it is likely that the AAIB will declare the flight illegal but the state of the upkeep of the plane and the precise cause of the crash are now lost in the waters off Guernsey. There were already concerns about the 35 year-old aircraft but Emiliano Sala's mother, Mercedes Taffarel, sister Romina and brother Dario accused the AAIB of letting them down in their search for the truth.

A statement released to *Telegraph* Sport on behalf of the family said they were "disappointed by the AAIB's response to Emiliano's death". It added: "They were especially surprised when, in the immediate aftermath of the incident, it appeared that the AAIB had given up on conducting a full search for the aeroplane, so it fell on them to do that. Without David Mearns locating the plane, Emiliano's body might never have been recovered and the potential significance of carbon-monoxide poisoning of him and the pilot would never have been known. The family still hope that the inquest process will provide them with the answers they seek in relation to Emiliano's death and that air safety will be improved, including the prevention of similar deaths in future. They hope that their faith in English justice is not betrayed. The family are keeping all options on the table as to their next move. They will do everything possible to ensure that the truth about this terrible accident is revealed, so no family has to go through the same torment."

In the AAIB's first bulletin, published in February, the prospect of the wreckage being salvaged was specifically mentioned, with the report stating that weather and sea conditions had made it impossible to recover it safely. Responding to calls to return to the site, it said doing so would "not add significantly to the investigation", which would "identify the correct safety issues through other means". It added that its decision had taken into account the "high cost" of a recovery and the risk that the wreckage "would not yield definitive evidence" following "a violent impact with the sea". One wonders if the AAIB would play down the evidential value of wreckage from a crash on land? In the end Cardiff City helped fund a fresh search for the wreckage in October which revealed that very little of it remained at the original site.

However the non-recovery of the plane is only one baffling aspect of this tragedy. There are many other vital questions still unanswered and there is plenty of evidence that is yet to emerge.

The role of David Henderson appears to be the key. His central role in arranging for his friend David Ibbotson to pilot the plane was originally believed to have been the catalyst for the tragedy. With Henderson currently on bail following his arrest in June on suspicion of manslaughter, the result of the police investigation may unearth several more twists and turns yet. Henderson's testimony is of vital importance and there is no doubt that the Sala family lawyers are exploring potential litigation depending on his answers to several key questions: who owned the plane that was apparently kept in such a bad condition that, according to the toxicology report, it effectively poisoned both pilot and passenger? Why was Henderson, an experienced pilot who has ferried similar single-engined aircraft as far as California, not behind the controls on that fateful night? What qualifications did Henderson think his pal David Ibbotson had to be at the controls in his stead?

Given that carbon monoxide has now been discovered as leaking into the cockpit. Other key testimony will come from the Trustors of the plane, a company called Cool Flourish, a management consultancy business.

In October 2019 a trial of consequence began following a *Telegraph* undercover operation into football corruption that threw up the name of Neil Warnock, raising further questions about the Cardiff boss's relationship with football agents. However, there is no suggestion that this has anything to do with Warnock's relationship with McKay. A "corrupt" football agent told the *Telegraph* undercover reporter that "if you can't beat them, join them" as a trial heard how a covert newspaper sting was "massively in the public interest".

Dax Price, 48, was recorded saying how the "trouble" with English football was that "everyone is getting looked after" as deals are brokered to secure lucrative player transfers, Southwark Crown Court heard. Price, along with fellow agent Giuseppe 'Pino' Pagliara, 64, were charged with paying and facilitating a bribe in the *Telegraph*'s 'Football for Sale' case.

Secret recordings of their meetings and telephone conversations with Claire Newell, the *Telegraph*'s investigations editor, were played to the jury during which it was claimed "backhanders" to managers were commonplace. The agents explained how Harry Redknapp, then Director of Football at Derby, and Cardiff boss Neil Warnock "needed looking after" while brokering deals. The football agent was also recorded explaining how the UK was where "everyone wants to be", adding how "there are so many ways of getting paid, different types of getting paid."

There were recordings of Pagliara saying that while he had operated in a "sneaky" way for 30 years, he was now eager to be "transparent", before telling the reporter that the football industry is "not for the faint hearted and it's not for the morally correct." Pagliara, from Bury, Greater Manchester, concluded: "If you've got those sentiments, respectfully change business." Price added: "That's the trouble – everyone is getting looked after."

Giving evidence on the third day of the trial, Ms Newell said in 2015 she received a tip-off from a source about club managers receiving "bungs and bribes" from football agents during player transfer deals. She told the jury of seven men and five women: "I thought it was massively in the public interest to expose this kind of behaviour because, on the face of it, it would appear to be quite straight forward corruption."

She explained how she set up a fake German-based sports company called Meiran which she pretended had wealthy Far East investors eager to cash in on football transfers. When the investigation was published in Autumn 2016, Sam Allardyce, the England manager, was forced to resign.

More than 40 football agents were investigated for breaking official rules over three years, the *Telegraph* reported following the publication of their investigation. Forty-two "intermediaries" had allegations against them looked into by the FA's disciplinary team. The details were contained in correspondence between the FA and a committee of MPs, raising questions about the scale of corruption in football. Figures provided by the FA showed that 42 cases involving "intermediaries" had been investigated between 2014 and 2017. Eight remained open at that time, 10 were proved correct. A senior MP said the figures showed how "widespread" the problem of rogue football agents was in the game and questioned whether the FA committed enough resources to tackling wrongdoing. Details of the cases came in a letter from Greg Clarke, the then newly-appointed FA chairman, to the Commons culture, media and sport committee.

Clearly, the court case examining 'bungs' in football, and naming Warnock, would not make for comfortable reading for the Cardiff City board in the middle of a fight to regain Premier League status.

Yet there was an enigmatic remark from Willie McKay at the height of the pressures on him over the Sala tragedy that if "he went down, he would take others with him!" From Cardiff's point of view, they have so much more to worry about, as top of their agenda was FIFA's written explanation of their findings upon which they would base their appeal to CAS.

Meanwhile the off the record feedback from FIFA's committee, the FIA, that neither Nantes nor the Welsh club had done a great deal directly for the family, hurt those at Cardiff who had wanted to help the family financially. Cardiff owner Vincent Tan had put up personal funds to repatriate Sala's body for the funeral to his home town, the club helped a second search for the plane wreckage near Guernsey and debated for some considerable time the best way to help the family and had been in constant touch with the family's lawyers.

Cardiff fans made it clear on social media they wanted something tangible to remember Sala by. Chairman Mehmet Dalman fully agreed with their sentiments and wanted to donate the first year of Sala's salary to the family, a hefty £2million. It was a noble idea but it would concede the argument that Sala was legally their player at the time the plane went down. As their legal battle with Nantes relies on Sala's legal status as a player still being in dispute, it was regarded as too big a risk to prejudice a case which the chairman admits could bankrupt the club. Instead Cardiff are putting together proposals for a Trust Fund in the family's name.

In November 2019 the axe finally fell on the Cardiff City reign of Neil Warnock. On the surface it seemed to have less to do with the tragic events of January 2019 and more to do with the Bluebirds' poor run of form which saw them stuck in mid-table several points adrift of the play-off places.

As Neil Warnock left the dressing after a derby defeat to rivals Bristol City, he knew it was time to inform chairman Mehmet Dalman that his time was finally up. "We had a chat, we've been so close, and I felt it was the right time and he agreed," Warnock said of his conversation with Dalman. "He agreed reluctantly because he didn't want me to go until Christmas but I didn't want it all to be soured. I've got such a good relationship with the fans and I just think it's the right time now, while everybody is singing from the same hymn sheet. It's a great club and they can move forward now with the new manager and that's what I want the club to do. I wish them every success."

Dalman gave his version of the decisive meeting when he said:

"It was Neil's decision to go. I really wanted him to stay until the end of the season but he felt it was time for a change. I think he was quite relieved when I had a chat with him and we felt it was right. He left on his own terms. He's been a great servant to the club."

When asked by a BBC Wales reporter whether Warnock had been sacked Dalman replied "Oh good god no!"

According to the chairman Warnock had never been the same since Sala's death. "I remember immediately afterwards that we were playing Southampton and I had prepared a speech in my mind to let Neil know how much we were supporting him." This was the point at which Warnock had publicly stated he felt like quitting. Dalman went on, "I wanted to tell him to 'man up' and tell him he would be okay but as soon as I saw his face I knew it was best to say nothing, or I might push him too much and push him over the edge. He was clearly affected.

"He has not been the same since the Sala incident, it might have been back in January but he had not really recovered fully, there is no doubt how much it has affected him."

Rumours of Warnock's departure had been rife for weeks as stories surrounding his refusal to surrender private text messages seemed to be causing a rift between club and manager. However it has now emerged that Warnock had belatedly agreed to cooperate with the club's request at the time of his resignation. Was this really a coincidence? Sources within the club suggest not as Warnock would have been aware that leaving Cardiff's employ would not have prevented the club from continuing their requests for sight of the texts and emails regarding the Sala transfer.

The source confirmed that the club didn't fire him, and certainly didn't fire him over the texts. In fact he had decided to cooperate. Whether he surrenders all the texts and emails relevant to the Sala transaction remains to be seen. However conspiracy theorists will make much of the timing.

Now approaching his 71st birthday and with only months left to go on the final season of his contract with retirement only months away, there seemed to be so many issues piling up that the wily old fox believed it was a good time to walk just before

Christmas and preserve his reputation as one of the most popular Bluebird managers in modern times.

Cardiff chairman Mehmet Dalman asked him to carry on, no doubt to give the club some breathing space and time to do their research on the next manager, although of course, they had already thought about Warnock's replacement.

Warnock left with Cardiff 14th in the table. The defeat to Bristol City came fast on the heels of defeat at Welsh rivals Swansea, and even his most hardened supporters had began to lose faith, with any hope of a quick fire promotion back to the Premier League now looking unlikely.

"I am leaving my beloved Bluebirds after over three years of which have been some of the best days in my long football career," Warnock said in his statement. "It is a shared belief that this is the right time for a new voice as we believe this squad of players is more than capable of getting success."

Warnock, who has been in management since 1980, was appointed Cardiff City manager in October 2016 and left the Bluebirds after 144 games in charge, with 59 wins, 29 draws and 56 defeats. In his second season with Cardiff he guided them to promotion to the Premier League, a record eighth promotion campaign for Warnock as a manager, although they were relegated after just one season in the top flight.

Dalman said in an official statement: "On behalf of Cardiff City Football Club, I thank Neil for his invaluable contribution to the future of this great club. He not only gained promotion but played a pivotal role in uniting the fans and the club. I am personally upset by his departure and wish him the very best for the future."

As well as thanking the Cardiff hierarchy, staff, players and fans, Warnock reserved special praise for the support of Dalman. "I would especially like to thank Mehmet Dalman whom I have said many times has been one of the best chairman I have had the privilege to work for. His support has been immense, especially in 2019 which for many reasons both on and off the field has been the most challenging period both emotionally and physically that I have ever encountered."

Warnock said the death of Sala had been "by far the most difficult week in my career" and the manager was all consumed by the fall out and the consequences, some of which came knocking were laid at his door. His relationship with Willie McKay, and his reluctance to hand over to his employers emails and texts involving the Sala transfer had surely hastened his exit.

Warnock's dealings in the transfer market involved players such as Gary Madine, Josh Murphy, Bobby Reid, and others, over their value for money, although player recruitment isn't an exact science and even the greatest managers are vulnerable to scrutiny when it comes to assessing value for money.

Bluebirds legend Craig Bellamy embarrassed Warnock by saying more home-grown talent should have been brought through by the manager when Cardiff owner Vincent Tan wants a business model where the best Welsh teenagers developed at the capital city club. With so much coming at Warnock from so many directions, little wonder a man who must have had one of the thickest skins in football could take it no longer.

17: EPILOGUE

CARDIFF'S OFFICIAL SUBMISSION TO FIFA contained numerous references to on-going criminal and possible civil litigation and their insistence that Nantes have a case to answer for negligence through their association with Willie McKay, the agent who booked the flight, and whose son Mark had the contract to sell Sala through his company.

McKay's association with manager Neil Warnock remains one of the cornerstones of the entire internal investigation being undertaken by Cardiff City. The Cardiff boss had tried to distance himself from the football agent which did not help the Scot's dark moods, and was a possible factor in his threatening outbursts while Warnock's reluctance to handover his text messages to the club's lawyers was a possible explanation for the popular Yorkshireman's resignation as Cardiff boss.

Repeated requests and refusals for access to Warnock's private messages, both texts and emails, were met with the legitimate response that they were of a private nature. In response the club suggested using an independent lawyer to filter the texts to remove any private communications and deliver only those messages in relation to the Sala transfer. That offer was repeatedly rebuffed by the Cardiff manager before he finally relented in the wake of his resignation. Those messages could put a fresh perspective on how the transfer was negotiated.

Meanwhile McKay's connection with Nantes is seemingly unimpaired despite the Sala tragedy. In November, in the week of what would have been Emiliano Sala's 29th birthday, speculation was rife in France that Mark McKay had come to an agreement with Waldemar Kita for the sale of defensive midfielder Abdoulaye Toure during the upcoming January transfer window. Nantes, riding high in the Ligue 1 table, were looking to boost their finances having not yet received a penny of the Sala transfer despite FIFA's ruling in September. It seems that while the precise details of the reasons behind the final tragic minutes of Emiliano Sala's life remain a mystery, football agents still meet chairmen, promote players, sweet talk managers, arrange flights and book hotels to watch the next big thing who might them a few quid because a manager sees the player as the difference between relegation and survival. Ultimately the game still relies on people like Willie McKay because, as he so eloquently put it in his original email to Emiliano Sala, "They [the agents] only care about money. That is the truth because that's all we care about. That's why we like to work for clubs - no emotion, simple business. That's it!" Despite the number of football clubs taking the long view and appointing Directors of Football, there remain old school managers who lean on people like McKay to save their skins during the frantic January transfer window.

A year on many questions remain unanswered and a large hole seems to be at the heart of any subsequent reports and legal cases in the shape of the lost wreckage of the plane. How can the aviation authorities, the coroner or criminal courts come to any hard and fast conclusions when so much evidence was lost? Surely it did not need to be that way given the more hospitable weather conditions that prevailed during the summer months.

In place of certainty we are left with speculation and, inevitably, conspiracy theories. In the privacy of Pall Mall clubs, during networking events, at convivial dinner parties or even within the boardrooms at some of the biggest clubs in the game, those closest to the facts have been debating some of the wilder theories. such as why did David Henderson, such a respected and experienced pilot, hand over the controls of the plane that carried Sala to a man seemingly desperate for money because he was in debt, someone who was a part-time pilot at best and who didn't have a licence to fly commercially?

Why has Henderson refused point blank to cooperate with Cardiff City when the club wrote directly to him, as well as his lawyers, requesting his help in unravelling certain facts to which only he knows the answer?

The Killing of Emiliano Sala

How is it that if David Ibbotson had one outstanding skill it was as a skydiver? And why was the pilot not in the plane when the privately-funded salvage operation discovered the body of the footballer, but not the pilot? Was the pilot able to unbuckle his seat belt and eject himself from the plane before it plummeted to its fate? If the pilot survived where is he? If he didn't survive, then where is his body? Predictions that Ibbotson's body might wash up on the coast of northern France have also proved to be false.

If there was foul play of some kind, who would have gained? Who else might have had a vested interest - it's well known within the football industry that there can be many secretive figures with an interest in a player as third parties? Who were these figures? Were they gangsters?

As for the police enquiries into criminal man-slaughter; what did Henderson tell the police, what will become of Cardiff City's litigation for negligence, liability and criminal manslaughter? What litigation will the Sala family pursue?

These are just some of the pertinent questions to which we are all still searching for answers: Was Emiliano Sala killed? And if so, why and who did it? Some of these speculations seem far fetched, but given what has already happened in this case - are they? Having listened to some of the conspiracy theories from those armed with information that has so far yet to come to light, it would appear their conclusion is that Emiliano Sala was the victim of foul play of some sort, and those responsible need to be brought to account..

One positive aspect of the whole tragedy has been that the Sala case has shone a light into the shadier aspects of the football world. Beneath the glory and the fame of the player lie dozens of dependants starting with the agents, player's families and friends and even, as we have seen, football clubs they played for when they were children. Emiliano was just one of over 50,000 footballers across the globe who got paid to play the game and, even though it was for the wrong reason, he will never be forgotten.

Emiliano Raúl Sala Taffarel - 1990-2019
REST IN PEACE

INDEX

Printed in Great Britain
by Amazon